GO FLY A SAILPLANE

GO FLY
A SAILPLANE

AN INTRODUCTION TO SOARING

RAY MORROW
LINDA MORROW

NEW YORK   1981   ATHENEUM

Library of Congress Cataloging in Publication Data

Morrow, Linda.
   Go fly a sailplane.

   1.   Gliding and soaring.   2.   Gliders (Aeronautics)
3.   Gliding and soaring—United States.   I.   Morrow,
Ray, joint author.   II.   Title.
GV764.M67   1981   797.5'5'0973   80-65995
ISBN 0-689-11080-4

Excerpts from the November 1977 issue of *Soaring* Magazine and the *1980
Directory of Soaring Sites and Organizations* are reprinted by permission of The
Soaring Society of America, Inc.

FOR KIM AND CHRIS

ACKNOWLEDGMENTS

We are grateful for the help of a number of generous people. Our thanks to Mike Moore and Mark Wild at Black Forest Gliderport; to Carson Lockwood, Bill Miller, and Squadron 8's Explorer Flight School; to Jim Foreman, who took photos and shared his experience in flying with us; to Tom Ward, who offered ideas for Chapter 4: Soaring Science; to Bob Spellman, who helped process and reproduce photographs; to Helen Berggren, who drew the illustrations; to Gunter Voltz, who rounded up contacts; to Schweizer Aircraft Corporation; to Shirley Sliwa and the National Soaring Museum; to John P. Dezzutti, Lianna Lamont, John Lee, George Uveges and the Soaring Society of America; and, of course, to the teenagers around the country who talked with us and shared their enthusiasm for soaring.

INTRODUCTION

An early morning sun baked the blackland prairies of northern Texas and, already, enormous woolly clouds floated overhead. Heat radiated from the gliderport's buildings and sent a mirage shimmering across the Caddo Mills runway. Seventeen-year-old Sherman Griffith and his mentor, national soaring champion Dick Johnson, trudged to separate sailplanes on the flight line. They carried parachutes, navigation charts, drinking water, and something to munch on. Passing up a poolside barbecue and other Fourth of July traditionals, the pilots had chosen instead a 300-mile out-and-return soaring task and were about to strike out for a third day of flying.

Sherman stowed his gear, pulled on his parachute, and lowered himself delicately into his sailplane. Quickly he ran through his preflight check: controls, OK; altimeter, reset; trim, flaps, seat belts, OK. Then he waited.

When his turn came for launch, Sherman's gleaming, white Nimbus II was hooked to the tow plane. He signaled that he was ready for takeoff. As the tow plane taxied down the runway, the Nimbus behind it looked ungainly at first, its 20-meter wingspan awkwardly seeking a bite in the hot summer air. But as the powered craft lifted off, Sherman's sailplane gracefully followed it into the sky. At 2,500 feet he yanked the release knob. Now he was on his own.

Spotting Dick's sailplane spiraling upward a mile away and 1,000 feet above him, Sherman headed for the same rising mass of air that his friend was riding to cloud base. After gaining all the altitude they wanted from the thermal, the pilots set off on their self-appointed course. First one leading, then the other, their twin silhouettes slipped across the sky. Borrowing lift wherever they found it and following magnificent cloud streets, they soared for most of the day.

When they reached their preset turnpoint, more than one hundred miles out, each pilot lowered a wing and turned around for the long trip back. Shadows lengthened in the late afternoon, and the sun, which had been their source of energy in the strong part of the day, began to lose its efficiency. Sherman and Dick circled under the last cloud left in sight, slowly working their way to 8,000 feet. Then they turned out of the thermal and headed for home, hoping they had stored enough "fuel" to make it in one, long, final glide. With Caddo Mills still forty miles away, they called upon all of the performance that had been designed into their ships and began the job of "edgin' it on."

After thirty-five tense but exciting minutes and with 500 feet of altitude to spare, both pilots entered the landing pattern and set their ships down on the runway. Sherman climbed out of the cockpit, his brown shirt striped with bands of perspiration, and savored a moment of personal triumph. In three days of holiday soaring, the budding national competition pilot and his friend had spent nearly twenty-five hours in the air and had flown over 1,000 motorless miles.

"It's fascinating . . ." he said. "It's the ultimate." Sherman Griffith is hardly your typical teenage soaring pilot. As he is quick to point out in conversation, he's had the advantages of

SHERMAN GRIFFITH

Sherman Griffith is one of the country's top soaring pilots.

exceptional coaching and expensive equipment. But he has discovered something that anyone else can find—the quiet freedom and exhilaration of soaring.

Go Fly a Sailplane is for anyone who has ever admired a motorless aircraft or held a "joy stick" in his hand and felt the immediacy of the atmosphere around him. It's for anyone who is looking for a new way to challenge him- or herself and has ever wondered what the sport of soaring is like. The book answers questions about how safe soaring is, how you can get involved without a lot of money, and how you can improve your skills once you're hooked. It also touches on the history of the sport, describes the training process, explains the science and aerodynamics of soaring, and profiles a number of remarkable young pilots who've already soared to heights of achievement. Read what they say about flying sailplanes; their stories will show you better than we can tell that soaring is special and that you can do it.

CONTENTS

xii   *Contents*

GO FLY A SAILPLANE

1

WHAT IS A SAILPLANE?

ON A SUMMER DAY in the Mojave Desert of California, a group of Explorer Scouts clustered at the end of an airstrip. They were learning to fly sailplanes and taking turns in the front seat of a beautiful, silver Blanik. After his demonstration flight one youngster, who was asked how he liked it, grinned and said, "It's like riding in a paper airplane."

Maybe it's the quiet simplicity of a sailplane that makes it seem toylike, or maybe it's something else. Without a motor or propeller it can stay in the sky for hours. Though it is tough and dependable, its wings come off to fit inside a trailer if its pilot lands out at the end of the day. Though it is flown with proficiency by keen, competitive pilots the world over, its handling can be learned by a novice. And though it is the result of man's ingenuity with design and materials, it constantly converges with nature.

If these seem like a puzzling set of features, let's look at the physics of flying to understand how a sailplane soars.

Staying Up Without an Engine

Although a sailplane turning and wheeling under the clouds may look like magic to the spectator on the ground, its capability isn't mysterious, and neither is it a helpless aircraft that hangs in the sky until that dreadful moment "when the wind stops." Wind doesn't keep a sailplane up; its own aerodynamics and a little help from nature do. The sailplane's design characteristics make it want to remain airborne. Of its own nature it glides at a very shallow angle and, once launched, returns to the ground very slowly. When a sailplane has been towed, say to 2,000 feet, it will coast down gradually, taking about fifteen minutes to return to earth. This is all made possible by the fortunate existence of an *airfoil*.

A sailplane's wing is constructed in a special shape known as an airfoil. It is designed so that the air moving along its upper surface exerts less pressure than the air moving along its lower surface. Lower pressure on top of the wing results in an upward force known as *lift*. The opposite force acting on the ship is *drag*, or resistance to its moving through the air. The faster an airfoil moves through the air, the more lift it generates. In a powered plane the engine creates thrust, moving the aircraft forward. In a sailplane gravity does. The sailplane, in its natural attitude, flies with its nose pointed slightly down. That way gravity produces the speed necessary to create lift.

On the other hand, when a sailplane pilot flies into another kind of lift, air that is going up, he goes up, too. Even though the ship is really coasting, it can climb in air that is rising, and the pilot can enjoy the exciting illusion that he is outwitting gravity. He is, in fact, soaring.

It's Safer than You Think

The question that a cautious newcomer always asks about youth programs in soaring is, "Is it safe to send a kid up in one of those things?" Perhaps the best answer is inherent in the Federal Aviation Administration (FAA) regulations that permit a

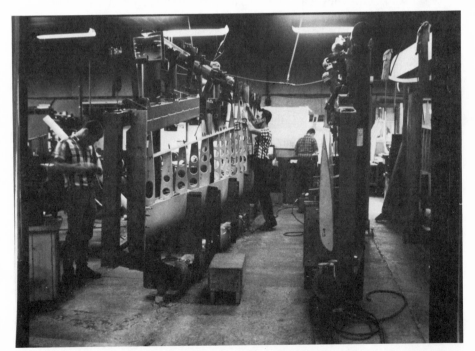

SCHWEIZER AIRCRAFT CORPORATION

Sailplanes are built in modern factories to exacting FAA standards.

fourteen-year-old to solo in a sailplane two years before he can take the controls of a powered plane or, in most states, even of the family automobile. Much of this agency's confidence in sailplane operation is based on the very absence of an engine. Without a motor a pilot needn't fear for its failure, and without a motor the pilot's training must be geared to the limitations of the aircraft. He learns to avoid situations that he couldn't handle without an engine, and he learns to plan his flights so that he is able to reach safe landing sites.

The construction of the sailplane is another aspect of its safety. Ships are designed especially for slow flight and are built more ruggedly than conventional airplanes you'll see at an airport. Not only can they land safely in unimproved areas off the runway, but they can withstand forces equalling many times their own weight. One sailplane design, for example, is stressed to 12 G's, or twelve times its own weight. Controllability is so precise that a sailplane can be brought down and stopped within the distance of a football field.

Certainly when you put an aircraft in motion, an element of risk is present, and sailplane accidents do happen. But the risk involved is precisely why professional instructors are dedicated to producing competent new aviators. The careful, sustained training program that every would-be pilot must complete is perhaps the best assurance of safety in sailplanes—this, and a careful attitude, according to Mike Moore, Director of Flight Instruction at Black Forest Gliderport in Colorado. When parents ask him how safe soaring is before they enroll their teenagers in his summer training camp, he answers with: "How receptive and responsible is your son or daughter? If he or she will pay attention to his learning and accept discipline, he's going to be safe."

Training offered by an FAA-licensed glider instructor in a dual-controlled ship takes the student from basic handling to emergency procedures. The idea is to simulate just about every condition that a pilot will encounter and to teach the student to react to it intelligently in a controlled environment.

What if you get into a storm? A sailplane pilot usually doesn't get into storms, because soaring is a fair-weather sport. You watch the weather forecasts and fly only in stable conditions. Before long, you will have become your own meteorologist as well, alert to the atmosphere as it changes around you.

SAILPLANE OR GLIDER—WHICH IS IT?

If you spend time around gliderports talking with soaring buffs, you'll notice that *sailplane* and *glider* are used interchangeably in their lingo, just as the terms will be in this book. But technically the words have different meanings. *To glide* is to fly forward through the air while losing altitude; it is the aeronautical equivalent of sledding. *To soar* is to fly without engine power while gaining altitude, or more poetically, to lift one's spirits and imagination far above the earth.

A sailplane is a glider designed especially for soaring. In the early days of flying, gliders had a limited performance that allowed them only to float or coast down from a high point of elevation to a lower one. But as aviation technology improved the glider, its sinking speed was decreased, and it became capable of gaining altitude in rising air currents. Since it could now do more than simply glide to earth, its name was revised to indicate a soaring plane, or a sailplane. And that's why soaring enthusiasts prefer *sailplane* to *glider*, just as they often choose the word *soaring* over *gliding*.

HANG GLIDERS SOAR, TOO

Perhaps because *hang gliding*, colorful and spectacular as it is, receives so much attention in magazines and television, people often confuse it with *soaring*. The two sports are actually quite different, as are *sailplanes* and *hang gliders*.

The hang glider is an aircraft that is smaller and slower than a sailplane. Without a cockpit or a stick-and-rudder control system, it is flown simply by the pilot's weight shift. Suspended at the apex of a triangular bar, he moves his body in the direction he wants to go. To cause the hang glider's nose to go down, for example, he moves forward; to go left he shifts his body to the left. Situated on a bluff or a hill, the pilot takes off running with the hang glider, then lies out prone once the "kite" is airborne. Quick and nimble, the hang glider can match the sailplane in many ways. It is capable of flying at 45 miles per hour (mph), soaring high above the earth—at record heights of 11,000 feet— and coasting twenty feet forward for every foot relinquished in altitude. It will cease to fly, or stall, at 15 mph.

But the hang glider is inferior to the sailplane in many ways, particularly in terms of safety. Because it normally flies close to the ground, it doesn't afford much room for error when recovering from spins or stalls. Since a judgment factor is critical in reading conditions and making tactical decisions, hang gliding can be treacherous to the casual newcomer. If you want to learn how to hang glide safely and responsibly, you must find an approved school at an excellent location and proceed with caution.

"L Over D" Means Performance

Two major forces act on the sailplane: lift, as we have seen, and drag. *The ratio between lift and drag describes the glide performance of a sailplane at a given time.* If the lift, for example, is twenty times as great as drag, the ship will travel twenty feet for each foot of altitude lost. In other words it will glide forward twenty feet while descending one foot. Expressed as "L over D" and written $L/D = 20{:}1$, this ratio defines performance. A pilot flying at the speed that gives the best L/D will be descending in the shallowest glide angle possible. The Schweizer 2-33 sailplane, which is commonly used as a trainer, has an L/D of 23 to 1. Sophisticated ships flown in competition may have a glide ratio of up to 50 to 1.

SCHWEIZER AIRCRAFT CORPORATION

The Schweizer 2–33 is a basic training ship, popular,
ruggedly built and easy to fly.

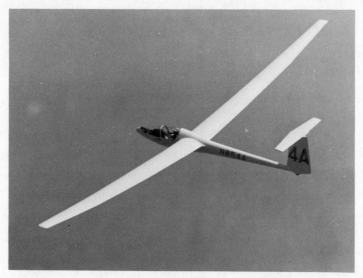

The Open Class, high-performance Glasflugal 604 is an expensive fiberglass ship with a wingspan of 22 meters and glide ratio of 49:1.

Good sailplane design will allow it to climb well in updrafts and "to penetrate," or maintain a very flat gliding angle even at high speeds. The amazing performance of the finest sailplanes depends on new, wing airfoils, longer wingspans, and very clean lines that minimize air resistance. It has been estimated that only two horsepower is needed to keep an efficient sailplane in level flight at 60 mph.

What happens without updrafts? When the pilot releases the tow cable and fails to find rising air, as is often the case, his ship will simply glide to earth. But not before giving him a leisurely and scenic ride on the way down. Until he is qualified to try cross-country soaring, the pilot will fly within easy returning range of the gliderport and begin his landing approach at 1,000 feet.

A THING OF BEAUTY WILL SOAR FOREVER

Airspeeds in a sailplane are much lower than those in a powered plane. A training ship may fly at 45 to 65 mph under normal conditions. A high-performance ship, in competition, will streak over the finish line at 150 mph. As for altitude, sailplane flights of nearly 50,000 feet have been made in mountain wave conditions, like those over Pike's Peak, easily exceeding the altitude of commercial jetliners. The world record for altitude soaring is 46,267 feet above sea level, or nine miles high. It was set by Paul F. Bikle in a Schweizer 1-23 on February 25, 1961, over Lancaster, California. A flight like this requires oxygen, of course, and even higher altitudes would make a pressure suit necessary. Normally, however, recreational flights by the beginner will range from 2,500 feet to 8,000 feet above ground level.

When a sailplane pilot flies into a rising column of air, he delights in a free ride. The lifting energy in such a column, known as a *thermal*, is capable of taking up a sailplane at 500 to 1,500 feet per minute (fpm). Sound like an unlikely elevator? On any summer contest day an ordinary thermal, containing literally tons of rising air, will lift a gaggle of up to thirty sailplanes. Another source of lift to the soaring pilot is *ridge lift*, created when a steady wind blows against a mountain ridge. Using a combination of thermals and ridge lift under ideal conditions, a pilot may stay up all day and cross several state lines. Karl Striedieck did just this, in fact, on May 9, 1977, when he flew across Pennsylvania, Maryland, West Virginia, and Tennessee. After more than fourteen hours aloft he had earned the world's out-and-return record with a 1,000-mile flight. Granted, it's a dramatic record that belongs to a champion, but flights of several hundred miles are quite common among weekend soaring pilots. In fact a sailplane can stay aloft as long as there is sunlight and lift. Staying up often comes down to a matter of the pilot's endurance. How long can he or she stay awake and confined to a space that is not as big as a bathtub?

Ford Motor Company once advertised its LTD model as "quieter than a sailplane," a reference resented by many soaring pilots who like to think of their ships as quieter than automobiles. Actually, a Schweizer 2-23 trainer isn't noiseless; you can hear fuselage creaking, cables moving, and wind rushing as the ship pushes itself through the air. But the slender high-performance sailplane is not unlike a championship diver whose lean style and skill allow him to slip cleanly into the water without a splash. The more streamlined a sailplane is, the less noise it makes in the air.

PILOTING THE SHIP

People sometimes have the mistaken impression that a sailplane floats aimlessly in the sky. They are surprised to learn that it can be maneuvered just as a powered plane can be: with a *stick* and a *rudder*. The stick, which is located between the pilot's knees, actuates the *ailerons* and the *elevator*. The ailerons, in turn, cause the wings to bank; the elevator controls the sailplane's up-and-down motion. Rudder pedals at the pilot's feet move the plane's nose left or right. By using these controls skillfully, a pilot can make the sailplane turn, dive, and, depending on speed, climb. He uses them to land too.

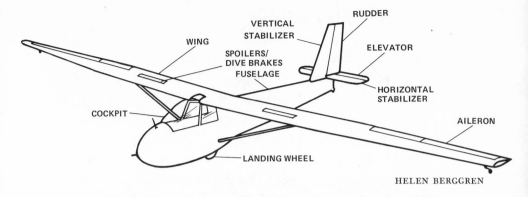

RUDDER
VERTICAL STABILIZER
WING
ELEVATOR
SPOILERS/ DIVE BRAKES
FUSELAGE
HORIZONTAL STABILIZER
COCKPIT
AILERON
LANDING WHEEL

HELEN BERGGREN

The trainer, like all modern sailplanes, is flown with a stick and rudder. Its aerodynamic control system is the same as that of a powered plane.

Every sailplane's touchdown on the runway has been carefully planned—usually at higher than 1,000 feet over the field—and is part of a deliberate maneuver. The pilot uses *spoilers* and *dive brakes* to aid in coming down. These are all devices that essentially spoil the wings' lifting characteristics and cause the sailplane to descend in a steeper glide path. It touches down gently with its nose in a low attitude, landing on one small wheel. "Getting the bird back home" requires careful training and good judgment on the pilot's part. He must plan his landing spot correctly, land on it, and then come to rest with a gentle application of the wheel brake. Most of the landing strip will still lie ahead when the ship comes to a stop, usually within seventy yards of touching down.

SPIT, POLISH . . .

A modern sailplane is more efficient than a powered plane because it has better lift characteristics and less drag, or wind resistance. In searching for less drag, sailplane designers have made the nose like a bullet and the cockpit small and narrow. With certain designs, they have even provided for the pilot to sit in a semireclining position and have replaced the bubble canopy with a sleek plexiglass cover that streamlines the fuselage.

But regardless of the canopy's shape, it is made to detach from the sailplane instantly in case of an emergency. Detachable wings and tail enable a pilot and his crew to disconnect the control linkages, to remove bolts and pins, and to lift each wing into a waiting trailer. The sailplane's light weight makes ground-handling easy for two people.

LINDA MORROW

A sailplane is designed to be disassembled for ease of transportation from one soaring site to another. Here Kevin Wayt removes the wing of his Zuni after a contest at El Mirage, California.

Before each flight, the canopy is washed and shined to remove smears that would spoil the view or hinder the pilot's vision on a late afternoon landing into the setting sun. A pilot will take great care, in fact, to clean and wipe down the entire exterior of his ship. It is a labor of love that can mean greater overall performance and that figures importantly in a soaring contest.

. . . AND PAGEANTRY

A sailplane is a beautiful creation to men and women who appreciate its delicate lines and amazing capability. But probably no sailplane owner has been more moved with pride and passion for his ship than Dick Huppertz. In 1977, after twenty-five years in soaring, he purchased a new, Romanian-built sailplane and named it *Nadia*, in honor of that country's champion gymnast, Nadia Comaneci, who dominated the 1976 Olympics.

GEORGE UVEGES

The Nadia, *a Romanian-built Lark, is towed to the flight line behind a Rolls Royce, after her christening at a desert soirée.*

With an air of humor and a dash of showmanship, he invited 200 guests to *Nadia's* christening, which was held outdoors at a desert gliderport in California. After two young girls performed gymnastic routines on a red-and-white balance bar and tumbling mat, a white convertible towed the red-and-white ship to the runway where a tow plane stood waiting.

Releasing from tow at 3,000 feet, *Nadia* and her pilot, a former soaring champion, flew loops, split S's and Cuban eights to music from "Nadia's Theme." It was a performance that thrilled Huppertz's hushed guests and lingered over them as they sipped champagne and dined in the gathering dusk.

EQUIPMENT AND COSTS

The basic price for a sailplane is $15,000 and up, but a number of extras are necessary. FAA regulations require that a sailplane be equipped with three basic instruments: *airspeed indicator*, *altimeter*, and *compass*. A serious pilot would also insist on adding a *variometer*, or rate-of-climb indicator. Other useful, though not essential, equipment might include a clock, an accelerometer, and a radio, not to mention oxygen tanks, navigational equipment, and special trailers for hauling the craft. Run a tally of these items, and you will realize that the handsome ship you admire on the runway may have had a price tag of $20,000 or more. Fortunately, secondhand sailplanes, ship rentals, soaring club membership, and joint ownership, as discussed in Chapter 11: Getting Started in Soaring, help to make the sport less costly.

Oxygen is required above 12,500 feet, but since training flights normally don't go that high, oxygen is rarely necessary. The pilot who hopes for a lofty adventure above this altitude, plans ahead by taking along oxygen equipment. A parachute is called for only when the pilot intends to perform aerobatics or to fly cross-country or in competition.

SOARING AND ECOLOGY

Many ecologists believe that soaring is ideal recreation. That's because the sailplane extracts its propellant from natural sources, uses no petroleum fuel itself, leaves behind no noxious fumes, and creates no sonic boom. But soaring does require some form of energy for launching, namely the aerotow, the winch, or the autotow. With energy in mind, many pilots believe that their sport will develop better use of the winch and the autotow in the 1980s in an effort to conserve aviation fuel.

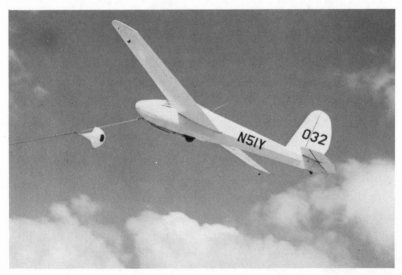

JIM FOREMAN

A winch launch takes this Schweizer 1–26 aloft at a steep angle.

LINDA MORROW

Self-launching sailplanes are becoming more popular because the pilot can use his retractable engine to get to soaring altitude. Mike and Aland Adams and a friend add fuel to their PIK–20E before a flight.

Another approach to soaring, likely to become more popular in the future, is the self-launching sailplane. This high-performance aircraft, known as a *motorglider*, has a retractable engine that the pilot can use to launch himself to what would normally be the *release area*. Here the engine is stopped and retracted, and soaring begins. If weather becomes a problem or if lift vanishs, the pilot can avoid an outlanding simply by extending his engine and flying toward better conditions. In addition to being an excellent trainer, the motorglider is capable of real soaring and of flying tasks comparable to those of motorless flight. In 1978 at the First European Motorglider Championships held in West Germany, 1,000 hours were logged between the start and finish lines; 975 of these were flown with engines stopped. Before the end of the meet, participating motorgliders had covered a total of approximately 24,000 miles, which nearly equals the distance around the earth at the equator, using only 3.2 gallons of fuel!

BUILDING YOUR OWN SAILPLANE

Although a beginner would not usually build his own ship, sailplanes can be constructed from kits or from sets of plans. The builder may purchase plans only, and then buy all the necessary materials, or he may order a set of prefabricated sailplane parts. In any case the home project is a demanding one that requires mechanical competence, precision wood- and metal-working ability, and basic knowledge of electronics. Several interesting home-built designs are available in kits.

JIM FOREMAN

The medium-performance Monerai, flying over Black Forest, Colorado, is one of several sailplanes available as a home-built kit.

Gliders in the Space Age

Sailplanes have been used over the years in the study of aerodynamics, a science that started with kites and gliders back in the days before power. This research has aided the development of high-lift wing airfoils as well as the reduction of drag. Currently, gliders are in fashion as "space hardware" and are among the reentry vehicles that the National Aeronautics and Space Administration (NASA) is testing. The space shuttle Orbiter *Enterprise* is a highly sophisticated glider, as was its predecessor, the M2-F1 Lifting Body. Looking very much like a schoolboy's giant paper glider, the space shuttle rides piggyback on a 747 jumbo jet, detaches at a calculated point in the maneuver, and glides back to earth.

NATIONAL AERONAUTICS AND SPACE ADMINISTRATION

NASA's Space Shuttle, The Orbiter Enterprise, *touches down on a dry lake following a simulated glide back from outer space.*

The space shuttle and super-capable airplanes like the one that carries it aloft came along some seventy-five years after the Wright brothers' historic work with gliders, which was centuries after humankind had begun to dabble with the notion of flight. Soaring—with its exotic ships and exciting opportunities —has come a long way, too. Let's look at how it all began.

2
BEGINNINGS

DAEDALUS IS THE famous architect and sculptor of Greek mythology who was commissioned by King Minos of Crete to build the Labyrinth, that puzzling network of passages. The king was so pleased with the Labyrinth that he wanted to keep Daedalus on the island as his resident genius. But because this arrangement made Daedalus feel that he was a captive, he yearned to escape by joining the birds in flight. So he began to study and explore how birds managed to fly. When he had finally figured out many of their secrets, he built for himself an elaborate set of wings, using feathers of graduating sizes and fastening them together with thread and wax.

When his young son Icarus watched Daedalus lift the wings and fly, the boy was ecstatic and wanted a pair of wings of his own. So Daedalus made a second set. He nervously attached the invention to Icarus and cautioned him. "Stay close to me, my son," he said, "and be wise. You must fly between heaven and earth and avoid the sun. If you come too close, it will scorch your feathers, and you will fall."

Then they rose to sample the skies together. People working in the fields and at sea looked up, astonished at them, and thought they were gods.

Delighted with his new power, Icarus would rise to a stunning height, and then swoop down again with great speed. But he became so thrilled with each exploit that, eventually, he forgot his father's warning and soared closer and closer to the sun. Suddenly the wax holding his feathers began to melt, and as they dropped away, he fell into the sea below and drowned.

The myth about Daedalus and Icarus does more than caution that every pilot must respect the limitations of his aircraft. It reminds us that humankind has always felt frustrated by his bonds to earth and has dreamed of flying. Wherever a set of wings are woven into the world's art and literature, the suggestion is freedom. But for hundreds of years, the freedom of flying was literally a lofty matter—that is, it belonged mostly to fantasy and speculation.

THOSE MAGNIFICENT MEN OF SCIENCE

It was not until the 1200s that Englishman Roger Bacon looked at the problem of manned flight analytically and discovered that light objects could float in air. Then, in the late 1400s Leonardo da Vinci, the brilliant Italian artist and inventor, began studying how man could fly. He conceived of simple parachutes, propellers, and helicopters, filling notebook after notebook with his drawings. He also turned his keen eye, which must have been like a stop-motion movie camera, to all sorts of flying creatures. He noted the muscles of birds, the power of their wings, and the way they maneuvered. Da Vinci was convinced that man could create a flying apparatus for himself if he copied certain elements in nature. That was why he suggested the bat as the perfect model to study to learn about flying. He reasoned that the bat's membrane-covered wings would work better than feathered wings because they allowed no air to pass through them. Looking back at Da Vinci's bat drawings, it becomes apparent how perceptive he was; they look very much like foot-launched gliders that came along 400 years later.

In the 1800s a handful of innovators began experimenting with theories of flight in a practical way. Sir George Cayley, a wealthy Englishman, was one of them. He first wrote articles on the principles of heavier-than-air flight in 1804 and later designed several fliers, one a *biplane* (an aircraft with two sets of wings, one above the other), another resembling a helicopter. But apparently he wasn't interested in flying any of them himself. On one occasion, for example, he employed his coachman as test pilot. The man, John Appleby, carried out the flight successfully but failed to be impressed. When he came down, he quit his job, saying, "I was hired to drive, not to fly."

Otto Lilienthal, in 1894, decided not only to fly but to create his own experimental site where he could work with Cayley's theories. When he heard that a canal was being dug near Berlin, Germany, he purchased the dirt and built a dome-shaped hill, 50 feet high in the middle of a field. He surmised that at the

Otto Lilienthal pioneered gliding flight in the 1890's by jumping from a hill he had built himself, barely visible in this picture.

top of this hill he would have easy access to currents of air and that by running along the crest, with one of his folding monoplanes strapped to his back, he would be able to launch himself into the wind, regardless of its direction. Between 1894 and 1896 he made over 2,000 flights, lasting from a few seconds to over a minute. Many of these were brief soaring flights as he managed momentarily to gain altitude.

Using evidence he had gathered from his experiments, Lilienthal became the earliest person to understand gravity as a source of motorpower and stability. He learned also the advantages of the *cambered*, or curved, wing over a flat surface, and he compiled the best aerodynamic tables available until the Wright brothers came along. In short he demonstrated that human flight was achievable. Although he became the world's first real hang glider pilot, his flying technique remained rather primitive. He had little means of control in the air because he could balance his craft only by frantic shifts of his body. In 1896 he turned to an advanced system for maneuvering that proved to be tragic. A gust of wind caused his machine to stall, and he was killed when it plunged to the ground.

In California, John J. Montgomery, a contemporary of Lilienthal, began building and experimenting with gliders in 1884.

John Montgomery flew innovative aircraft like this glider
in California before the turn of the century.

He didn't need a conical hill because most of his flights took place near the coast outside San Diego, benefiting from a steady wind off the Pacific Ocean. Later, when he moved his aerial laboratory to Northern California, Professor Montgomery and his assistant managed to get their glider lifted into the air by way of a hot air balloon. One aircraft was towed to 4,000 feet and cut loose. During the twenty minute trip down, the kite-like contraption maneuvered in all sorts of spirals and figure eights that the local newspaper called amazing. A subsequent Montgomery flight ended, however, in a crash that was fatal to its pilot, Daniel Maloney.

GETTING IT WRIGHT

Aeronautical pioneers had already learned a great deal about manned flight before 1900. But because no one had figured out a means of controlling the aircraft adequately, many of these early innovators, as we have seen, paid for technical advances with their lives. Wilbur and Orville Wright investigated the problem of maintaining equilibrium further than anyone else had. By adapting the biplane design of Octave Chanute, they worked out the landmark *three-axis control system* (the up-and-down, side-to-side, and banking motion of the aircraft) that made flying safer than ever before.

On the sand dunes near Kitty Hawk, N. Carolina, the Wrights set up a spartan camp that consisted of a glider hangar and a tent. Meticulously they began testing the aerodynamic problems of balancing and steering an aircraft. Up to now, the pilot had hung from his glider and controlled it by shifting his weight from side to side. But this had little effect on the machine's attitude and direction. It still went pretty much where the wind took it.

The Wrights' first modification was to put the pilot into the glider in a prone position. This change alone made flying safer and also reduced the drag created by the pilot hanging from the glider. But now the pilot couldn't launch himself by running; he had to rely on a ground crew. Up to this time, there was no concept of *lateral control*, that is, turning the aircraft left or right. The Wright brothers were careful students of soaring birds and noticed that all soaring birds make changes in the shape of their wings to control their lateral equilibrium. What the Wrights did was to adapt the birds' behavior to their test glider, the Flyer, and change the shape of the wing in order to increase lift on one wing, while decreasing lift on the other wing. They accomplished this by warping the edge of the wings by means of cables operated by a *control stick*. To turn left, for example, they would increase the lift of the right wing, causing it to rise, and then decrease the lift of the left wing, causing it to lower. This banked the Flyer, causing it to turn.

Although the *rudder* had been developed earlier to control the left-to-right alignment of the airplane with the airstream, the Wrights understood and developed the coordinated use of stick and rudder to effect a banked turn in which the airplane is neither slipping nor skidding through a turn. The development of these interrelated control techniques was the breakthrough that meant, for the first time in history, a pilot would be able to direct his aircraft in flight. It also provided the basis for all aircraft control systems that have been built ever since.

The Wright Brothers worked out the basic principles of aerodynamic controls on their 1902 flyer, just one year before they added an engine.

NATIONAL SOARING MUSEUM

In a third development, they added an *elevator* to the front of their glider that moved the nose up or down. Now they had constructed in place a three-axis system that controlled *roll*, *yaw*, and *pitch*. Twice they found themselves in the kind of stalls that had killed Lilienthal, but instead of diving to the ground, their machine settled easily onto the dunes.

Now they were ready to construct a powered machine. So they built a glider with enough wing area to support the extra weight of a power system. Then they added a four-cylinder engine and a propeller to their Flyer, and everyone knows the rest of the story. When they flew it successfully on December 17, 1903, the world had its first practical airplane.

During the next few years, the brothers continued to develop powered aircraft, but they returned to Kitty Hawk occasionally to fly their gliders. In 1911 they succeeded in making several sustained flights, the longest lasting nine and three-quarter minutes. It became the world's soaring record and stood for ten years.

NATIONAL SOARING MUSEUM

In 1911 the Wrights set a soaring record of 9¾ minutes that stood for ten years.

Neither the two inventors nor observers at the time quite realized the impact of their studies. But what Wilbur and Orville Wright had learned with gliders was the secret of controlled flight by humankind, which was to become the pivotal point for twentieth-century aviation.

HIGHLIGHTS AFTER KITTY HAWK

1911   German university students established the first summer soaring school and encampment on Wasserkuppe, the highest peak in the Rhön mountain range.

1919   The Treaty of Versailles, ending World War I, prevented Germany from flying powered aircraft. Instead the *Luftwaffe* turned to flying gliders and channeled their creativity into soaring.

1920   The first competition at Wasserkuppe attracted twenty-five different aircraft flown by sports-minded aviators across Europe.

1921   *The Blau Maus*, the *monoplane* (aircraft with only one pair of wings) glider flown by Wolfgang Klemperer, broke the Wright's record by soaring for thirteen minutes.

1922   In Germany *The Vampyr* became the first powerless aircraft to break the world's one-hour barrier for staying aloft.

1928   A visiting group of German soaring pilots demonstrated their sailplanes and soaring knowledge to Americans at Elmira, New York.

W. Hawley Bowlus designed and built the first real American sailplane in which Anne and Charles Lindbergh both achieved their C-level soaring certificates and badges.

The *variometer,* a rate-of-climb indicator, was invented. It was a breakthrough to soaring because it allowed the pilot to know when he had found the lift of a thermal.

1930   Soaring great Wolf Hirth discovered the technique of *thermaling,* or circling upward within a rising current of warm air. He covered forty miles in what was America's first cross-country flight.

The city of Elmira, New York, hosted the first U.S. National Soaring Championship.

1932   Soaring enthusiasts in Germany flew record one hundred-mile flights and reached altitudes of 10,000 feet. The Soaring Society of America was formed, becoming the coordinating agency for gliding and soaring activities in the United States.

1937   The first World Soaring Championship was held on Wasserkuppe in Germany.

1940–45 Gliders were used as military cargo planes during World War II. They were loaded with men, jeeps, and howitzers and allowed to glide silently to the ground behind enemy lines. However, many German and American pilots were killed when these operations failed.

Early Launching and Learning

Using a "bungee" cord as a giant rubberband, early soaring buffs launched each other for brief flights.

Compared to being towed aloft by a snappy Super Cub—a typical scene at gliderports today—early launching methods were quite primitive. Pilots of the historic hang gliders, like Lilienthal, launched themselves into the wind by running down a hill or jumping off a small bluff. Later gliders, which were larger but very lightweight, used a different method we could call *the slingshot launch*. An elastic shock cord, much like a giant rubber band and called a *bungee*, was attached to the nose of a glider. Men on the ground took both ends of the shock cord and ran as hard as they could downhill. When the cord was stretched to its limit, the ship would be released to leap into the air. After the glider landed at the bottom of the hill, it had to be carried back up again by way of ground crew power.

Ralph Carter, with the help of his brother and a friend, built a glider in 1911 at the age of fifteen. The boys had been inspired when pioneer aviator Glenn Curtis landed his powered biplane, by chance, in a neighbor's field near Omaha, Nebraska. So they used the Curtis machine as a model and turned it into a glider. They made the frame of spruce, and used linen dipped in paraffin and alcohol to cover the wings. "I was the smallest of the three," Carter remembered, "so I was the first to fly it. We used a horse to pull it into the air the first time; then we used a motorcycle."

RALPH CARTER

Ralph Carter built and flew a glider in 1911 at the age of fifteen.

Anyone with an automobile in those days could hook a glider to it at the end of a long cable and watch his craft lift into the air as the car accelerated. Another early method was by *winch launch*. Here a cable extended between a motor-driven winch and the glider. When the winch reeled in the cable fast enough, the glider reached flying speed and was up and away.

The best and safest means of launching proved to be by *airplane tow*. This method was demonstrated by Frank Hawks in 1930, when he had a biplane to tow him across the United States from San Diego to New York in his Franklin *Eaglet*. By way of aerotow—then as now—the glider could climb into the air at the end of a 200-foot-long rope behind a tow plane and then release at any altitude the pilot wished.

Learning to fly in the early days was largely by trial and error. Because two-place ships didn't exist yet, the student had no way of enjoying the luxury of an instructor sitting behind him, ready to take over if things got shaky. Instead, his introduction to flying gliders took place in a *primary*, which basically was a wing, a tail, and a sticklike fuselage. Wearing his cap bill backwards so it wouldn't fly off in the wind, the pilot/student sat in an open cockpit, just ahead of the wing. After a few dry runs on the ground to teach himself what the controls could do, he was flung into the air by his friends on the shock cord. His teacher remained earthbound, crossing his fingers and waving his arms.

Eventually the so-called utility glider was improved to become a two-place dual-controlled ship. This *trainer*, an ancestor of the Schweizer 2-33, allowed the instructor to teach from a seat behind the student and to take over the controls when necessary. Learning now became more effective and flying much safer.

GLIDERS OF METAL AND GLASS

In time the sailplane has evolved from a crude and stubby tomboy of a ship to a slender nymph. Early gliders were constructed of peeled willow for a frame, which was covered with cotton cloth and bonded glue. The Germans developed an all-metal sailplane. Later on a combination of metal frame with metal-and-fabric skin was used and is still seen today. But the newest and most dramatic change in sailplane construction is fiberglass. This method sandwiched balsa wood between glass cloth and resin. The result is a very strong but lightweight material that can be molded, sanded, and painted. By using a master mold, the builder can reproduce any number of sailplanes, each as smooth and flexible as the last.

As they learned more about aerodynamics and materials, designers over the years have unveiled dozens of sailplanes. Here are a few important ones:

The *Minimoa* was the gull-winged sailplane designed by Wolf Hirth. The American altitude record in 1936 was set in this ship at 19,434 feet.

The *Zanonia* was designed, built, and flown by Harland Ross in 1937. With this ship, the first to exceed a glide ratio of 30:1, John Robinson held the National Distance Record for nearly ten years and set the World Altitude Record (at the time).

The *RJ-5* was the first ship to reach a 40:1 glide ratio. It used an advanced airfoil derived from studies carried out at the University of Mississippi in the early 1950s. It was the first ship to exceed a flight of 500 miles, a World Record for twelve years, and in it, four national championships were won.

THE RICHARD MILLER COLLECTION, COURTESY SOARING SOCIETY OF AMERICA

The vintage Nimimoa, designed by soaring great Wolf Hirth,
set an American altitude record of 19,434 feet.

The *Schweizer 1-21* was the first competition sailplane built entirely from metal. It won the U.S. Nationals six weeks after it was built.

The *Schweizer 2-22* was the trainer in which many current pilots cut their teeth. It was constructed from a rugged steel-tube fuselage with fabric covered aluminum wings. Although its performance is modest, it is a good climber with a tight turning radius.

The *Schweizer* 1-26 was developed as a fun and inexpensive, single-place ship. Small, nimble, and responsive, it became an American favorite; there are 700 of these sailplanes flying. Since the performance of all 1-26s is identical, it makes for very even soaring competition.

SCHWEIZER AIRCRAFT CORPORATION

Most soaring pilots make the transition to Schweizer's single-place 1–26 after training. Designed for low-cost sailplane simplicity, the 1–26 provides one-design competition similar to sailboat class racing.

The *Libelle, Daimant,* and *Phoebus* were the first generation of fiberglass sailplanes, appearing in the early 1960s. They came along after designers had learned how to reduce drag by minimizing frontal areas and putting the pilot in a semireclining position. Their canopies were smoothed into the lines of the fuselage to give them a sleek look and higher performance.

The slender and graceful Standard Libelle is a high-performance, fiberglass ship often flown in soaring competition.

SAILPLANES AND RESEARCH

Because of their light weight and slow speed, sailplanes are well suited to probing turbulent air. They can ride the very *wave currents* (powerful air mass movements that occur downwind of a mountain ridge) being studied and measure them more simply without engines. The Sierra Wave Project and the Jet Stream Project were research efforts shared by the U.S. Air Force, Navy, and Weather Bureau and were begun near Bishop, California, in 1951. A team of meteorologists, including seven sailplane pilots, studied the wave in the lee of the Sierra Nevada Mountains. During the four-year project, pilots recorded altitudes ranging from 24,000 to 40,000 feet. In one incident a Pratt-Read, one of the strongest sailplanes ever built, was destroyed in the turbulence of a *rotor cloud* (a rotating air mass). Pilot Larry Edgar parachuted to earth, although he was injured, and later made the following notations about the wreckage of his ship: "Nose pulled off at the seats . . . left wing broken off . . . tail boom broken cleanly from fuselage . . . control cables leading from nose to tail pulled apart in a bunch. . . ." The force required to do this damage was estimated to be over 10,000 pounds. Research data resulting from these projects have allowed meteorologists to warn airline pilots and other aviators of rotor conditions and thus to minimize dangers of this vicious phenomenon.

FLIGHT IS FREEDOM

In what may seem a real-life version of Daedalus and Icarus in the space age, newspapers carried an account of a daring glider flight in early 1979. An East German engineer escaped to the West by flying a glider over the fortified border and landing at a British military air base. Observers said he was flying at less than 125 feet as he slipped into freedom across the border at Gatow and settled his ship down in West Berlin.

3

THUMBS UP!
YOUR FIRST FLIGHT

AT LAST IT'S YOUR TURN for a demo ride in a sailplane. Alongside your pilot, you walk toward the waiting, two-
place trainer, its canopy open as if to beckon you. Your pilot
offers you the front seat, and you climb into the narrow cockpit.
He swings into the seat behind you, helps you wrestle with the
shoulder harness, and asks you to latch the canopy.

Outside a line boy hooks up the tow rope, then waits at one
wing tip. You give him the thumbs up signal, and he raises the
wing to hold your ship level. Up ahead, you see the tow plane
rudder wag back and forth, asking if you're ready. Your pilot
steps on the rudder pedals one at a time to answer yes.

The tow plane's engine revs up for takeoff and so does your
pulse rate. The sailplane rolls forward, being dragged down the

Just before her demo ride, this passenger/student waits with her pilot/instructor to close the canopy.

RAY MORROW

LINDA MORROW

Sailplanes line up waiting for the tow plane on a busy weekend at a glider port.

runway at speeds a good jogger could match. Shuddering at first, then lifting off its single wheel to float behind the tow plane, it climbs toward the sky.

From inside the cockpit, you watch the whole world spread out beneath you, a tableau of tans, greens, and indigos. In moments you are detached from all that lies below and drawn to a new way of looking at things. You stare down at the tops of trees, a patch of alfalfa or a desert dotted with sagebrush.

Suddenly you feel a quick, sinking sensation in your stomach and find yourself grabbing for a handle. The whoop-de-doos you

LINDA MORROW

The tow plane ahead, like an eager wasp, tugs your ship skyward.

ride on tow for a moment are caused when the ship hits potholes that lie unseen in the air.

A gentle whoosh of wind presses against the sailplane as it follows the tow plane higher and higher. At 2,000 feet your pilot asks you to reach for the big red knob on the control panel and to pull it. With a great *thwang* the tow cable detaches and trails out before you. The tow plane falls away to the left and your ship veers into a climbing turn to the right. Now it's alone and free in the sky.

The world seen from a different angle spreads out below as you sight along one wing.

LINDA MORROW

Now you're alone in the sky and looking for lift.

The ship banks to one side, its instrument panel reflected on the canopy.

Your pilot offers you the *control stick* so you can try your hand. Push it to the left, and the ship rolls into a bank to the left. Pushing it back to the right first brings the ship level and then lowers the right wing. Easing it forward lowers the nose of the ship; pulling back raises it again. It's easy. You move the stick the way you want the sailplane to go.

Suddenly the air outside comes to life, and the sailplane surges under you. Your pilot, with interest in his voice, says, "Here, I'll take it," as the needle on the altimeter begins winding up—2,500 feet, 3,000 feet. You're in the midst of a *thermal*, and you can feel its lift with the seat of your pants. Now the needle gauges 4,000 feet, and still you're circling upward, borrowing energy from rising air beneath you. Perhaps, as you spiral and turn, you see a hawk who has joined you to share in the same natural elevator. You look out on a special moment in space and sense the adventure of soaring.

How to Get a Ride

Newcomers learn about soaring by knowing a pilot, from reading about the sport, or simply by watching sailplanes drift in the sky. One person we know, for example, was traveling along a highway when he saw the sun glinting off the white wings of a sailplane as it slowly circled overhead. The motorist became so intrigued that he turned onto a side road for a closer look. He soon came upon a hand-lettered sign offering glider rides, found the site where the craft had been launched, and met a pilot who took him up for a sailplane ride on the spot.

You too may take a spur-of-the-moment ride if you find yourself near a gliderport. You may, on the other hand, know an acquaintance or relative who is involved in soaring and would take you up for the asking. But aside from these possibilities, you can check on soaring opportunities in your area by referring to Chapter 13: Where to Soar in the USA, or by contacting: The Soaring Society of America, P.O. Box 66071, Los Angeles, CA 90066; (213) 390-4447. This organization will give you the name, location, and telephone number of one of the eighty commercial operations nearest you in the United States. The Soaring Society of America (SSA) may also give you the names of certain soaring club members, if such a group operates from the local gliderport, who are certified flight instructors and who may be available to offer you a ride at a reduced rate.

Becoming a member of the SSA is an excellent way to learn about the sport. The Society, of approximately 15,000 members in the United States and abroad, acts as a central information source for people interested in soaring and provides many special services for its members. Full-time students aged twenty-two and under pay annual dues of $18; a full membership costs $28.

Student membership in the society includes:

Subscription to *Soaring* magazine, the monthly journal of the SSA and the only periodical in the United States devoted exclusively to the sport of soaring. It highlights soaring competitions, homebuilding hints, flight stories, performance evaluations, safety articles, and general membership news.

SSA membership card and decal of SSA emblem

FAI Sporting License, which permits the holder to participate in officially sanctioned competitions and earn international soaring proficiency badges

Professional representation and liaison with the Federal Aviation Administration and the Federal Communications Commission (FCC) to preserve airspace rights and flying privileges for soaring pilots

Safety and training programs designed to upgrade the quality of soaring instruction and the overall safe enjoyment of sport soaring. The official SSA Ground School Program offers a course that may be studied individually or in a classroom situation. It includes text, with workbook sections, final exam and answer sheet, and a copy of a sectional chart.

Plus . . .

Group sailplane hull and liability insurance

Privilege of electing representatives to the SSA's Board of Directors

Special membership discounts on selected merchandise

Eligibility to establish state soaring records

Free insurance of A, B, C, and Silver, Gold, and Diamond Badges when earned

Comprehensive soaring film library maintained by the National Soaring Museum

Free listing of used sailplanes for sale

Annual membership meeting and soaring convention

Recorded after-hours soaring information phone service

Since soaring and cities normally don't go together, gliderports are located out in the boondocks, and you may face a long drive. That's why it's best to phone ahead to reserve a demonstration flight before you leave home.

Clerks and dispatchers keep a gliderport operating smoothly.

LINDA MORROW

The operations clerk at the soaring site will schedule a flight time for you, along with a ship and pilot. If you have a tendency toward motion sickness, which an occasional passenger notices on his first ride, you can protect yourself by taking a Dramamine or Bonine tablet about an hour before your ride. If it's a perfect, sunny soaring day, you may want a camera, cut-off jeans, and a hat. Otherwise, no extra preparation is necessary. After all, soaring is simplicity, remember?

Your first flight will last twenty to thirty minutes and will cost approximately $25. Yes, it is expensive, but you are paying for three costly items: sailplane rental, tow plane service, and professional pilot/instructor.

After your introductory ride you can assess your reaction to soaring and decide if you want to take lessons. If the answer is yes, you'll want to purchase your own copy of *The Glider Pilot's Log Book* at the gliderport and ask the pilot who just took you up to log your first flight. It's a beginning and will count toward your accumulation of experience in the cockpit. In your log book will be recorded each future flight you take, remarks on your progress and, eventually, your pilot rating, should you solo.

What's in It for You?

If you decide to take flight instruction and to aim for a glider pilot's license, challenge and reward await you. We'll talk about the challenge in Chapter 8: How to Get a License. The reward is a new self-reliance that comes with knowing you are competent in the cockpit. Here are a few comments from observers who often watch students in the process of becoming pilots:

"I know of no other single endeavor that can better aid a person in maturing than learning to fly a glider."—Dan Matzke, flight instructor and psychologist.

"It's a constant learning experience. . . . It's incredible how much there is to know about soaring and how long it takes to learn it, but doing it well is a big confidence builder."—Scott Imlay, national junior soaring competitor.

"Soaring is a great medicine. Once you master this sublime thing, it's a great source of satisfaction."—Frank Borik, flight instructor and Explorer Scout adviser.

PEOPLE AT A GLIDERPORT

The pilot who is responsible for taking you up may also end up being your flight instructor. His or her proficiency has been certified by the Federal Aviation Administration after he has earned a commercial pilot's license with a glider rating and an instructor's rating and has demonstrated his ability to teach. Chances are that he loves flying and enjoys helping students through the learning process of mastering a glider. And if he or she is anything like one instructor we met at Estrella Sailport in Arizona, you'll get more than your money's worth. This fellow likes to show the glider's capabilities in maneuvering and also to point out that hiking trails on the hills below reveal fossilized seashells as proof that a prehistoric ocean once covered the area. He often adds too that his own favorite pastime is to strike out for Tucson, some one hundred miles away, soaring in thermals across the sky, and flying back home again before dark. Like so many other soaring pilots, he is turned on to nature, probably because he has learned to cooperate with it.

Then again, perhaps your pilot/instructor will be as uninhibited and joyful about his avocation as Leo Smothers, a teacher in Iceland who roams the globe on school holidays, flying every chance he gets. When you go up with Leo, you have to be ready for enthusiasm. He keeps up an animated explanation of how he's going to demonstrate a stall and perform other maneuvers and where to look for signs of lift. While he hunts for a thermal, he may coax the needle on the variometer by thundering, "Come on, baby, give us a ride!" And whether he's able to

Flight instructors Leo and Mary Smothers pull a silver Blanik from a field of wild flowers onto the runway during a soaring "busman's holiday."

climb at 500 fpm or not, he's delighted just to be in a sailplane. Back on the ground, he's been known to lift the canopy, throw back his head, and holler, "Whoopee . . . !"

The tow plane that launches your ship is typically a Citabria, a Piper Super Cub, or a similar "tail dragger." The pilot at its controls must be an FAA-certified commercial pilot with an instrument rating. This is an advanced pilot rating that permits a pilot, when flying a properly equipped aircraft, to fly at night or in clouds. The pilot must also have shown his familiarity with techniques and procedures essential to safe towing. He has taken this job perhaps because he wants to log hundreds of hours to qualify for training in a flying career—say, as an airline pilot—or, perhaps, like an orthodontist in Texas, because he enjoys piloting small airplanes. A boring job? Maybe. But can you think of a better way to hone your skills at taking off and landing?

The atmosphere of a commercial glider operation is low key compared to an ordinary airport. Air traffic is much lighter and fewer people are on hand, except during competitions. Often the operations shack is a modest office in a mobile home or an A-frame. But inside, efficient clerks keep track of flight

LINDA MORROW

Sailplanes tied down along the flight line seem beckoned
by an inviting Colorado sky.

scheduling, making sure you get a sailplane and a tow, and maintain radio contact with sailplanes in the air that are so equipped. Instructors meet a steady stream of students, and pilots of privately owned sailplanes check in before taking their equipment out. It's a good place to meet interesting people and to overhear a bit of "hangar flying," the legendary tale-swapping that goes on among soaring pilots.

On the day of your "demo hop," arrive early so you can check in leisurely and look over the operation. Take a walk through the hangar or along the runway, where a collection of private sailplanes are usually tied down. Many are sleek and streamlined, others are vintage and well worn. Taken all together, they are as varied and colorful as sailboats bobbing in their slips at a marina.

4

SOARING SCIENCE

LIFT

AS A SAILPLANE slowly glides along, wheeling and turning in the still morning air, it appears to hang motionless on some invisible thread. What actually supports the sailplane is something called *lift*. Lift is created by air flowing smoothly over the wing. The wing is designed so that air flowing over the top of the wing has lower pressure than air flowing over the bottom of the wing. We call this difference in pressure *lift*.

Lift is created by two different effects, each produced by air acting on the wing. The first effect is the result of the wing having a slight angle relative to the direction of air flow over the wing and is known as the *angle of attack*. This element of lift is

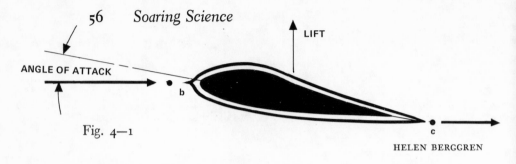

LIFT

ANGLE OF ATTACK

b

Fig. 4—1

c

HELEN BERGGREN

Cross section of an airfoil showing flow as it streamlines around the airfoil.
Note that lift is always perpendicular to the wind direction.

generated because *the air striking the angled underside of the wing is deflected downward, pushing the wing upward.* You can see this effect when you put your hand out the window of a moving car. Hold your hand out flat, palm facing down, toward the street. If you turn your hand to a slight angle with the wind, your hand will be lifted up, or pushed down, depending on which way you turn it. In a sailplane we are interested only in upward lift, so the leading edge of the wing is always angled up. This is called a *positive angle of attack.*

The second and more important component of lift is expressed by Bernoulli's law, named for the Swiss mathematician and hydrodynamicist. You can see from the illustration (Figure 4-1) that the wing is shaped like a slightly flattened teardrop, its upper curved surface longer than the lower. Since air particles moving from point *b* across the top of the wing have to reach point *c* at the same time as those traveling over the bottom of the wing, air on top must flow faster. Bernoulli discovered that when air travels faster, its pressure decreases; that is, *faster flowing air means lower pressure. Air flowing across the bottom of the wing creates higher pressure, and the resulting difference in pressure is what makes the wing fly.*

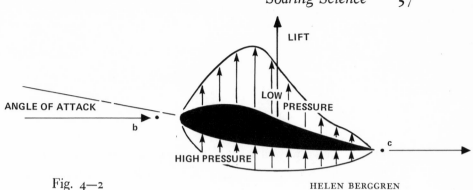

LIFT

LOW PRESSURE

ANGLE OF ATTACK

b

HIGH PRESSURE

c

Fig. 4—2

HELEN BERGGREN

Distribution of pressure on a wing is due to flow over the airfoil.

Bernoulli's principle can be demonstrated at home. Take an ordinary teaspoon and hold it loosely between your thumb and forefinger so that it can easily swing forward and back. Put it near a running faucet with the curved back nearest the water. When held a quarter inch or so away from the running water, the spoon hangs vertically, indicating that the pressure on both sides is equal. As you move the curved back of the teaspoon into contact with the water, water flowing over the curved surface of the spoon creates a lower pressure than the air, and the spoon is literally sucked into the water. Since Bernoulli's principle is true for gases such as air, as well as for liquids such as water, this simple experiment shows the amount of lift that can be produced by even relatively slow flow over an airfoil.

Fig. 4—3

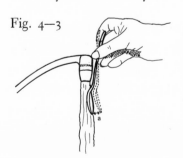

Demonstration of Bernoulli's Law. Fast flowing water over the back of a teaspoon lowers the pressure on that side, causing the spoon to "lift" into the water stream.

STALL

As angle of attack is increased, lift is also increased, to a point. At high angles of attack, the flow over the upper wing begins to separate in such a way that the wing begins to lose its efficiency. If the angle of attack continues to increase, the separation moves forward on the wing and reduces lift, until at some critical angle of attack the flow separates completely from the upper surface and the wing *stalls*. When the wing stalls, it no longer produces sufficient lift to support the sailplane. When flying in level flight, a stall usually causes the nose to drop sharply until the angle of attack is reduced sufficiently to reestablish the flow over the wing. *The only time a wing stalls is when it has exceeded its critical angle of attack; it does not depend upon airspeed or flight attitude.*

DRAG

As we have seen, lift is the good news. It supports the wings, which in turn support the rest of the sailplane, allowing us to fly. But, also associated with lift is drag, the bad news. *Drag is caused by resistance to the airflow over the wings and around the fuselage.* Drag is more complicated than lift because it originates from several different sources. It is caused by the shape of the aircraft, the smoothness of the surface, the aerodynamic design of the wings, and as a byproduct of lift generated by the wings. Total drag of a sailplane is due to the combination of

wing drag and *parasite drag*. Wing drag is the sum of two additional components: *profile drag* and *induced drag*.

Let's define each of these terms:

Total drag is resistance to the sailplane moving through the
air from all sources.

Profile drag is resistance caused by the wing moving through
the air *without producing lift*. It is caused primarily by flow separation along the top of the wing, called *pressure drag,* and by
resistance to the air moving across the wing's surface, called
skin friction. In a well-designed airfoil, skin friction is the largest
component of profile drag.

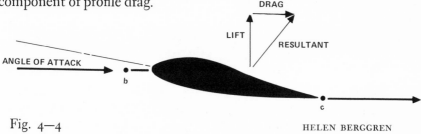

Fig. 4—4   HELEN BERGGREN

*Induced drag is a byproduct of lift. It is perpendicular
to lift and parallel to the airstream.*

Induced drag is a byproduct of lift, as shown in Figure 4-4.
When you stick your hand out of the car window and angle it to
produce lift, as we suggested, you can feel the increased drag as
well. When the angle of attack increases, you can feel the increased drag pushing your hand back.

Parasite drag is created by parts of the sailplane's fuselage
other than lifting surfaces of wing and horizontal tail. One component of parasite drag increases with increasing angle of attack,
while the other is fixed and has to do with how the ship's de-

signer has exposed rivets, struts, and fittings to the airstream.

Let's sum up what we've said about aerodynamic forces on sailplanes:

Lift is produced in reaction to air being deflected downward due to angle of attack and to low pressure produced by air flow over the upper surface of the wing.

Drag is the sum of several components and can be expressed: *Total drag* = (*profile drag* + *induced drag*) + *parasite drag*.

PERFORMANCE

As we soar high above the earth snug in a warm cocoon of rising air, we tend to ignore yet another force at work on our sailplane—*gravity*. In time, soaring conditions change, air cools, and gravity tugs us relentlessly back to earth. We can extend our time aloft in one, long, final glide, but gravity forces us down at a known and predictable rate.

In any sailplane there is a best speed at which to fly that will allow us to travel the greatest distance with minimum loss of altitude. This speed varies depending upon *lift*, *sink*, and *wind speed*. In general you slow down in lift and speed up in sink. As it turns out, the best glide angle of a sailplane in quiet air is determined by the ratio of the aerodynamic forces acting upon it; that is, lift divided by drag, written L/D and pronounced "L over D." In a trainer the best L/D is about 23:1 in still air. Although this L/D is determined from the ratio of aerodynamic forces, it is also the ratio of horizontal to vertical speed or the ratio of distance flown to each foot of altitude lost. This means that we can glide twenty-three feet forward for every foot of altitude we lose. From an altitude of only 2,000 feet we have almost 200 *square miles* from which to choose a landing site! In actual practice, however, this theoretical best L/D is seldom achieved, due either to wind, lift, or sink encountered en route or to slight flying errors that make the sailplane less efficient. These factors must be kept in mind when planning a flight or when estimating the distance to the gliderport or to a selected landing site.

SAILPLANE CONTROLS

Many of the flight problems encountered by aviation pioneers were caused by the difficulty in controlling their gliders in flight. The Wright brothers were the first to understand the need for controlling an aircraft in all three axes of space. What these historic innovators accomplished was to control separately an aircraft's motion in *pitch, roll,* and *yaw.*

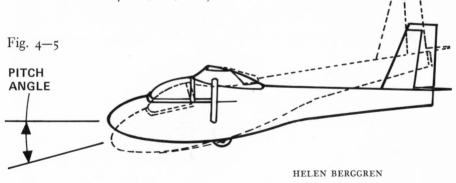

Fig. 4—5

PITCH
ANGLE

HELEN BERGGREN

Pitch controls the attitude about a sailplane's lateral axis.

PITCH

Pitch is the up-and-down motion of the sailplane's nose and is controlled by the elevator. When the control stick is pushed forward, the nose pitches down. When the stick is pulled back, the nose pitches up. *Pitch* is motion about the sailplane's *lateral axis* as shown in Figure 4-5. In a sailplane pitch controls the angle of attack of the wing as well as the angle of descent, and therefore the speed of the craft.

ROLL

Roll is the banking motion of the sailplane and is controlled by the ailerons on the wings. When the control stick is moved to

Fig. 4—6

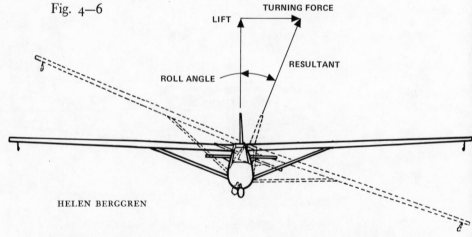

HELEN BERGGREN

Roll controls the bank angle about the sailplane's longitudinal axis.

the right, the right-hand aileron moves up, forcing the right wing down. At the same time, the left-hand aileron moves down, lifting the left wing up. This banking action, called roll, is what allows a sailplane to turn. *Roll* is motion about the sailplane's *longitudinal axis* as shown in Figure 4-6.

When the wings are banked, the lifting force of the wings is also banked, since the lifting force is always at right angles to the wing. This banked lifting force can be divided into two forces as shown. One force pointing straight up is the *vertical lift*; the other force pointing horizontally is the *turning force*. As you can see, the steeper the bank, the greater the turning force.

Fig. 4—7

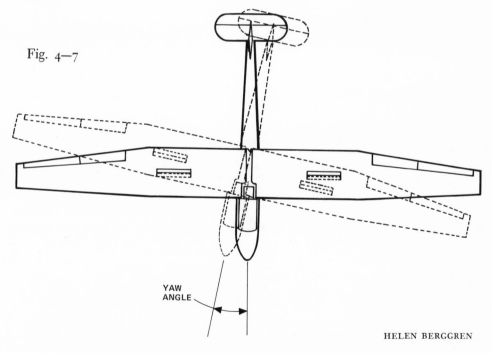

YAW ANGLE

HELEN BERGGREN

Yaw controls the side-to-side movement of the ship's nose about the vertical axis.

YAW

Yaw is the side-to-side movement of the sailplane's nose. It is caused by turning the rudder to the left or right. (The rudder does *not* turn the sailplane. See discussion under Roll. It is used in a turn, but only to coordinate the turn.) Yaw causes the sailplane to be misaligned with the airflow—that is, to skid sideways. *Yaw* is motion about the sailplane's *vertical axis* as shown in Figure 4-7.

5

SOARING WEATHER

A SAILPLANE OR GLIDER is always gliding downhill. In still air it has a very gentle rate of descent, losing only about 200 feet for each minute of flight. But air is rarely still for very long. In some places it is moving down; in other places, moving up. The art and sport of flying sailplanes is finding the *upward moving air* called lift, and avoiding the *downward moving air* known as sink. Soaring begins when you are gliding downhill in air that is rising faster than you are going down. If you successfully stay within this rising air, you can shortly gain thousands of feet in altitude.

This upward moving air mass should not be confused with the aerodynamic lift generated by an airfoil or wing in a moving airstream. Obviously, the wing must produce lift or we would drop

like the proverbial rock. *Lift in soaring refers to upward movement of the surrounding air.*

Soaring is a game of skill in finding lift, requiring that you
know what causes it and where the best places are to look for it.
Three main sources of lift we need to know about are *thermal
lift*, caused by warm rising air; *ridge lift*, caused by wind being
deflected upward by some natural obstruction such as a hill, cliff,
or mountain ridge; and *wave lift*, caused by disturbances in a
moving air mass downwind of a mountain range. Let's look at
these types of lift more closely to understand them and to learn
how they are used to support a sailplane.

THERMAL LIFT

Thermals, as you might guess, have something to do with heat.
As a bubble of air is heated, it expands, gets larger, and becomes
less dense than the surrounding air. Just like a hot air balloon,
the heated mass of air begins to rise. *This rising, heated mass of
air, called a thermal, provides the sailplane necessary lift to stay
aloft.*

In the early morning hours before the sun rises, the surface of
the earth and the air adjacent to the ground are at a uniform
temperature. There is usually little wind then because of this
equilibrium between air and land temperatures. As the sun
comes up, it begins to heat the ground unevenly. Surfaces that
face the sun heat faster than others, dark surfaces faster than
light, dry surfaces faster than wet. These differences all com-
bine to cause a differential heating effect, such that a paved
black asphalt parking lot, for example, will heat up much faster

than a recently watered golf course, even though they are getting the same amount of sunlight. As the parking lot absorbs the sun's energy and heats up, the air in contact with the parking lot surface also heats up and becomes warmer than the surrounding air. This warmer air expands and becomes less dense and, therefore, buoyant compared to the adjacent air. At some point, called the *triggering temperature*, the air contains enough heat energy to break free of the surface and begins to rise like a bubble. This air will continue to rise as long as the air temperature inside this bubble is warmer than the surrounding air.

Members of a ground crew near Jackson Hole, Wyoming, eye thermal-forming cumulus clouds while waiting for a tow.

GEORGE UVEGES

Meanwhile, back at the parking lot, cool air rushes in from all sides to replace the warm air that just left the ground on its way to becoming a thermal. This new cool air will undergo the same heating phenomenon caused by being in contact with the warm parking lot surface. It will expand, and then begin its own journey aloft. If the combination of temperatures, weather conditions, and surfaces is just right, a steady stream of warm air will rise over each thermal source. Often, however, the heating rate is inadequate to produce a steady upward flow of air and, in this case, the thermal pulses and intermittently sends a puff of warm air skyward. If we fly into one of these thermals and immediately circle within it, we can ride it up as far as it goes.

As the thermal rises, the air within it expands and cools. At some point, depending upon exact weather conditions of moisture and temperature, once-warm ground air cools to the *dew point* (the temperature at which vapor starts to condense) of the water entrained in the air and precipitates out as a cumulus cloud. In many places the existence of these cumulus clouds is one of the most reliable indicators of the location of thermals.

A natural change in temperature occurs with increasing altitude. Normally the higher the altitude, the lower the temperature; mountains are generally cooler than valleys. The rate at which the temperature changes with altitude is called the *lapse rate*. As long as our rising thermal is cooling at a rate less than the lapse rate, the temperature of our thermal will be higher than the surrounding air, meaning that it is less dense than the surrounding air so that it will rise even higher. This process continues until the temperature within the thermal is in equilibrium with the surrounding air, although the actual behavior of a thermal is a good deal more complex than the simplified explanation given here.

Cloud Streets

On certain days, when conditions of temperature, weather, and wind are exactly right, thermals will form in parallel rows like rows of corn. *An aerial photograph shows a cloud street to be continuous rows of puffy cumulus clouds, evenly spaced and aligned with the wind.* Under each cloud is a rising thermal providing endless lift for a sailplane. Many a soaring pilot has had the flight of his life along these cloud streets, traveling mile after mile at high speed without needing to stop or circle in lift to regain altitude.

Parallel to the rows of lift in the cloud street are rows of sink, in which the air is cascading to earth. These areas of sink are to be avoided if possible, or to be flown through fast so as to minimize the loss of altitude.

Ridge Lift

Whenever wind blows against an obstacle, such as a hill, a stand of trees, a cliff, or a mountain ridge, wind is deflected up, over, and around the obstruction. *Soaring pilots have long been accustomed to flying in this deflected airflow known as ridge lift.* A steady ocean breeze, blowing against the bluffs at Torrey Pines just north of La Jolla, California, has been home to two generations of soaring pilots who have been content to fly back and forth along these spectacular sea cliffs. Sailplanes now find themselves sharing this airspace with dozens of hang gliders as well as radio-controlled model sailplanes.

GEORGE UVEGES

*A Schweizer 1–23 soars the ridge lift above the bluffs
off Torrey Pines, California.*

On a larger scale a fine group of expert soaring pilots, known as the Allegheny Ridge Runners, regularly fly the ridge lift generated by easterly winds blowing against the Alleghenies. The world's out-and-return soaring record, in fact, was set on these ridges by Karl Striedieck when he flew his AS-W-17 from Lockhaven, Pennsylvania, to Oak Ridge, Tennessee, and back, covering a distance of over 1,000 miles in a single day without an engine.

As the wind approaches a ridge, it is deflected upward and over the ridge or slope. At low wind speeds the deflected layer of air doesn't move very fast, except close to the ridge. This requires flying close to the terrain on relatively weak days. As wind speed picks up, the turbulent layer of air next to the ridge becomes

Fig. 5—1

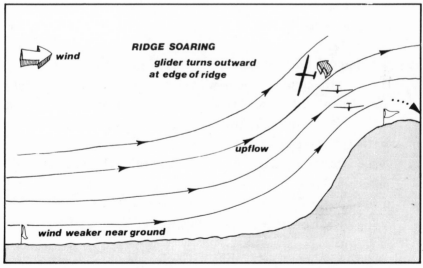

*Air flowing over a ridge provides pilots with outstanding
soaring opportunities in the rising air.*

thicker, and the deflected air mass also becomes thicker and moves faster. This allows the sailplane to fly further from the ridge and faster.

The best lift is typically obtained in front of and above the ridge crest, often at a 45° angle above the crest. As the wind rises up to clear the ridge, it often curls down on the lee side of the ridge, causing severe turbulence and sink. A sailplane pilot who finds himself below the crest on the lee side of the ridge is often trapped; it is nearly impossible for him to work his way back over a ridge once he is downwind and below the crest. Successfully flying ridge lift requires good knowledge of local wind conditions and ridge patterns; understanding of the rules-of-the-road; and strict attention to potential landing sites, airspeed, and lift. It also requires the new pilot to fly much closer to the terrain and to other traffic than he may be used to. Often the wing of his ship is just a few spans away from the ridge itself, and he may find himself flying in close company with several other sailplanes.

Before the pilot encounters a break in the ridge, or the end of the ridge, he must decide how to deal with the reduced or zero lift encountered there. Usually, it is best to reverse direction with a 180° turn while still in good lift along the ridge before getting to the end, or break. *For safety all turns on a ridge are made into the wind and away from the ridge.* This prevents the pilot from being blown into the ridge or downwind of the crest while making his 180° turn. Ridge soaring can be fun and exciting, but it is very demanding flying and requires a high level of alertness.

WAVE LIFT

A wave is one of nature's most awesome soaring phenomena. It contains enormous power that must be dealt with cautiously and on its own terms, but it also contains great beauty. Sitting alone in a sailplane cockpit in the eerie quiet and silky smoothness of a mountain wave is one of the high adventures of soaring. A *wave occurs downwind of a mountain range when weather*

A wing runner holds the glider level for seconds at the start of a winter wave flight.

JIM FOREMAN

conditions are just right. The wind must have the proper velocity, direction, and duration. The change in wind speed with altitude is also a factor, as are air temperatures aloft and the shape of the mountain.

What is a *wave?* When a pebble is dropped into a pond, it generates *ripples* that radiate out from the central point. These ripples are small waves, or *displacements,* in the water. Similarly, a boat tied up at anchor bobs up and down as *ocean waves* pass the boat. It is important to note that in these two instances *the wave is moving through the water; the water itself is not moving.* When we drop a pebble into a pond, the ripples, or waves, reach all the way to the shore, moving through the water with very little resistance. In a moving stream of water, we often encounter waves of a different sort. If a smooth flowing stream flows over a submerged log, for example, water will rise over the log and then cascade down the back side, undulating in a series of waves formed downstream of the log. These waves are called *standing waves,* just the opposite of ripples in a pond or the ocean wave described above. In this instance *water moves through the waves, while the waves themselves stand still.*

Standing waves can form in the atmosphere as well, downwind of a mountain range. The Sierra wave that forms in the lee of the Sierra Nevada Mountains over the Owens Valley in California and the wave forming in the lee of the Rocky Mountains over Colorado Springs, Colorado, are two well-known waves. Soaring flights above 40,000 feet have been made in both waves. *In addition to a required ridge or a mountain range with a steep lee escarpment, the atmosphere should contain a stable layer sandwiched between two unstable layers.* An unstable layer of air at low altitude will have a high lapse rate, that is, a relatively large drop in temperature with increasing altitude. In a middle stable layer the change in temperature with altitude is very small. Above this is another unstable layer, which, again, has a high lapse rate.

As a stable air mass flows over a mountain range it begins to move in a series of waves downstream of the mountain. Often, but not always, the existence of the wave is shown by a series of distinctly lens-shaped clouds downwind of the mountain, as shown in Figure 5-2. These *lenticular clouds* (called *lennies*)

Fig. 5—2

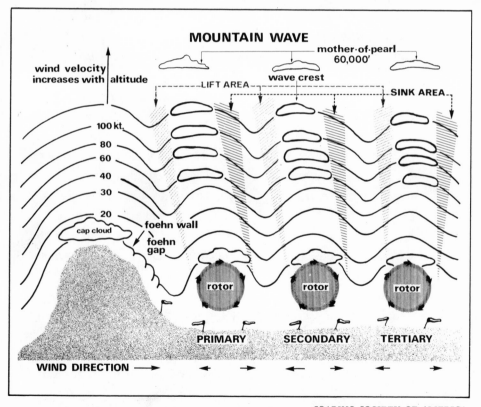

SOARING SOCIETY OF AMERICA

Anatomy of a wave, source of most high-altitude soaring flights.

appear to be stationary but, in fact, are continually forming at their upwind edge and evaporating at their downwind edge. These clouds generally mark the crest of the waves. The best lift is found just upwind of these lennies, while the heaviest sink is found just downwind of them. Interestingly, the clouds themselves do not indicate the strength of the wave but only the moisture content of the air and the condensation level. Best lift is often found high above lenticular clouds.

Two factors must be given careful consideration when flying a wave. One is the existence of a *rotor*, or rotating air mass, trapped between the upward moving air of one wave and the downward moving air of an adjacent wave. The rotor is often rough, occasionally violent, and can produce surface winds that make for difficult landing beneath one. *Don't venture into a rotor by accident; it's no place for beginners.*

A second factor is the *cloud cover* in the vicinity of a wave. Often there is a cap cloud over the top of a mountain range. Downstream is a clear area called a *foehn gap*. (*Foehn* is a German word meaning an Alpine south wind.) Changes in temperature or humidity can cause the lenticular clouds to extend both up and downwind and quickly change into a solid overcast, except for the foehn gap. When flying a wave above the cloud level, a pilot must keep an eye on the "windows" between the lenticular clouds. *Upon any indication that these windows are starting to close, the pilot must take steps to get through the openings before they close.*

Sailplanes must be specially equipped for cloud flying, and pilots must be instrument-rated before attempting to fly in clouds. Wave flying is not to be self-taught. Many soaring areas have small local waves that are easy and fun to fly. If the wave is working, have an instructor check you out before you tackle it on your own. Major wave areas are Black Forest, Colorado; Minden, Nevada; and Bishop, California. Each offers wave camps that provide in-depth training as well as proper equipment for high altitudes.

6

STUDENT AT THE STICK

IF YOU'VE NIBBLED at the thrill and beauty of soaring with an introductory ride but feel uncertain about committing yourself to a learning program, you'll want to know that most soaring centers offer a mini-course of three flying lessons for approximately $65. This gives you a large sample of the real thing and allows you to apply the fee toward a complete course if you decide to undertake one within twelve months.

But if you've flown in a sailplane and said to yourself, *"This is for me!"* you will want to know about the training required to qualify as a pilot and how to get into it.

No previous experience is necessary and requirements for learning are practical questions: Can you state that you have no known physical defect that would make you unable to pilot a glider? Are you willing to study basic aviation materials in a ground school or on your own? Can you provide a few hundred dollars over several months to fund your training? Will you be fourteen years of age before solo flight? If your answer is consistently yes, then your next step is to schedule a convenient time for a lesson at a commercial glider school.

The commercial operator is in business to offer you sailplane rental, FAA-certified instruction, and tow service, most likely aerotow. Although rental rates will vary at different locations around the country, a student should expect to pay $15 to $20 per hour for a two-place trainer. He will be charged around $14 an hour for the expertise of a flight instructor. And he will also have to pay the tow fee, which is $7 to $11 for the typical 2,000-foot tow. Totaling these costs, an hour's training session with two flights may cost $30 to $50.

How much training is required? Most instructors feel that thirty to thirty-five flights, or ten hours of dual instruction, are needed to prepare the student for solo. Thus the cost of learning to fly a sailplane generally ranges from $500 to $800, roughly the price of a motorcycle or a stereo. Most soaring centers, however, try to take the edge off training costs by offering beginners a complete package course, or "block time," that is somewhat reduced. This means that the student who contracts with an operator for a complete series of lessons through solo can save approximately ten percent.

How long does it take? At a soaring school where you can participate daily, your instruction can be concentrated, and you may be able to solo within two weeks. The weekend student, on the other hand, may take three to four months if he has a lesson every week or so and will bolster his own progress by studying flight theory and technique. People learn to fly more rapidly, of course, with continuous training that avoids long gaps in instruction. Instructor Dan Matzke enjoys working with people through the anxious struggles of mastering a sailplane. He makes this comment about the learning process: "Someone who is willing to spend time at home thinking about soaring and studying progresses faster and more enjoyably than the person who simply says, 'Teach me to fly.' " You'll find specific training texts mentioned in Chapter 8: How to Get a License, and under Further Readings. But for now, let's look at what your lessons in the air might be like.

No matter who teaches you to fly, he or she will necessarily be a certified flight instructor licensed by the Federal Aviation Administration to instruct students in the sport of gliding. Typically, he or she is an accomplished pilot with hundreds, if not thousands, of hours in all types of gliders and aircraft.

Your first lesson is likely to be scheduled in the morning when the field is uncrowded and the air calm. It starts with a discussion of the traffic pattern at the gliderport. Your instructor describes the direction in which gliders take off and land and the pattern that they fly in approaching the field for landing. Out on the field where a Schweizer 2-33 waits tied down, he walks you through the preflight check, working his way clockwise around the ship and pointing out what to check for.

Any veteran aviator will advise you never to get into an aircraft unless you believe it to be safe and airworthy. While it is often difficult to satisfy yourself in the case of a commercial airliner on which you've purchased a ticket, it is much easier to do with a sailplane. And given that the sky and natural elements that work on a ship are very unforgiving, the pilot must learn to

Dave Bigelow conducts a preflight check of his sailplane to assure himself of its airworthiness.

LINDA MORROW

check his ship, building into the experience a factor of safety. A missing bolt, a popped rivet, or evidence of leaking fluid are all signs of hazard and require attention.

The preflight check consists of removing gust locks that prevent wind from banging the controls against the stops, checking freedom of movement of the controls, checking to make sure the control rod ends have safety locks or pins at each connection, and assessing the general airworthiness of the sailplane. You must check to see that the previous pilot hasn't left any unwanted ballast in the cockpit. If you are light enough to need ballast, in order to meet the aircraft's minimum pilot weight, this is the time to add it, in the form of metal bars that are se-

*Instrument panel on a home-built Duster has gauges
to "read" altitude, air speed and lift.*

cured in place. Check to see if seat cushions are suitable for you
and adjust the rudder pedals and safety harness, and your "preflight" is complete.

After ground check a line crew moves the ship to the runway
in preparation for takeoff. Your instructor talks to you about
what your first lesson will involve, and then you both get into
the ship, buckle up, and get ready for takeoff. On the instrument panel in front of you are a number of gauges and small
plaques. You will notice an altimeter that shows the height of
the sailplane above sea level, an airspeed indicator that tells you

how fast the sailplane is moving through the air, and a variometer showing how fast the sailplane sinks or rises in relation to the surrounding air mass.

One of the most important yet simple instruments in a sailplane is a six-inch piece of yarn taped to the canopy—the *yaw string*. During the first few flights, you may suspect that its function is just to embarrass you, because it tells you when your flying is not coordinated. Any imprecision in your technique shows up when the yaw string is blown to one side or the other. If it points straight back, it indicates that you are flying well. If it points to the left or right, it shows that the sailplane is slipping or skidding sideways, not flying as efficiently as it was designed to.

The first of two information cards on the dash gives *per-*

Checking the tow cable is a safety must before each flight.

formance limitations of the sailplane: *maximum speed, weight,* and *maneuvering speed.* The other is the *takeoff checklist* that you learn to go through before each flight. It reminds you of the following:

Altimeter	Set to field elevation.
Belts	Fasten and adjust.
Controls	Check for proper operation; close and lock spoilers; set flaps.
Canopy	Close, check latches carefully.
Cable	Hook up, check release, and hook up again.
Direction	Observe direction of the wind.

The line boy or line girl with the end of the rope tow signals you to open the release. As he attaches the cable, you signal him to raise one wing, indicating that you are ready for takeoff.

UP AND AWAY

The instructor sitting behind you is now in full command, but remember that in the process of teaching you, he will gradually turn the ship over to you. Flying on tow, he holds a position just a few feet above the ground until the tow plane takes off; then you follow the tow plane to 2,500 feet above the field. From the air he points out traffic patterns used in your landing approach, along with various features of the local terrain and areas to avoid, if any. As soon as you release from tow, your instructor makes a climbing right-hand turn; the tow plane makes a diving left-hand turn to clear the area.

Once off tow, the instructor slows the ship to a gliding speed of 45 to 50 mph and checks to be sure there are no other aircraft

Learning to identify features around the gliderport is part of learning to land.

in the vicinity. Then he asks you to take the controls and follow him as he puts the sailplane through several maneuvers. He makes a 90° turn to the left by pushing the stick to the left and pressing the left rudder pedal at the same time. You notice that as the sailplane turns, the yaw string remains absolutely centered, indicating that the turn is coordinated and that airspeed doesn't increase during the turn. He then lines up with a certain feature on the ground—a highway intersection or a water tower—and asks you to make a 90° turn on your own. The object is to turn out from one heading and complete the turn on the other heading, 90° away. As you move the stick to initiate the turn, you may find it difficult to coordinate stick movement with rudder and to keep the yaw string centered during the turn. Practice will improve your skill.

As your instructor puts you through a series of left turns and right turns, repeating the exercise over again, it may seem that every other word from him is *coordination*, for proper use of the stick and rudder in combination is the secret to safe and efficient flying. It is well worth all of your effort to learn this valuable skill.

STRAIGHT FLIGHT

Flying a sailplane in straight flight would seem to be the easiest thing in the world, and in some ways it is. If you take your hands off the stick and your feet off the rudder pedals, the sailplane will fly itself. But unfortunately it goes where the wind wants it to go. With a side wind it drifts to the side; a little turbulence and its wings tilt and start to bank. So straight flight requires constant minor corrections on the pilot's part to maintain a heading, and is, surprisingly, more difficult than the turns. For one thing, you must maintain a *visual attitude reference* with the horizon at all times. This means knowing where the horizon is in relation to the instrument panel and wing tips. If, when you look to the side, one wing tip is below the horizon, you know you are in the process of turning in that direction, even though you can't tell it otherwise. As you look ahead over the instrument panel, the horizon should be slightly above the nose of the sailplane. If it's halfway up the wind screen, the nose of the sailplane is too low, and your speed is too great. If the horizon reference is below the instrument panel, it indicates that the nose of the sailplane is too high and that you are flying too slowly, making it extremely difficult to control the ship.

After fifteen to twenty minutes of air work, your sailplane will be down to 1,000 feet altitude and your instructor will take over the controls, showing you the proper *pattern entry*, the point at which you approach the landing field. Observing traffic in the area, gliders on the ground, and wind direction and velocity, he takes a *physical reference point* in the airport vicinity

Fig. 6—1   HELEN BERGGREN

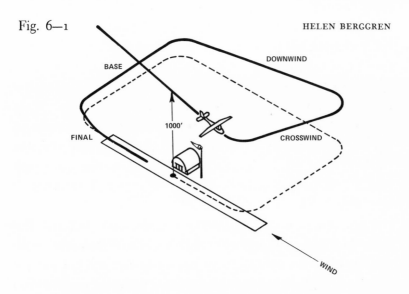

The drawing illustrates a four-sided landing pattern used at many gliderports.

for pattern entry. He explains that you want to be over this point with a minimum altitude of 600 to 800 feet. As he flies along the length of the runway observing traffic patterns, he makes a 90° turn and starts the crosswind leg taking him to one side of the airport runway, from which he makes another 90° turn to the downwind leg. At this point you should be able to look out of the canopy and see the runway at an angle of about 25° below the horizon. Once past the desired landing point, your instructor initiates a 90° turn onto the base leg. He deploys spoilers and dive brakes as necessary to adjust the sailplane's altitude and to control the glide slope for landing. At about 300 feet altitude, he initiates another 90° turn onto final, which lines the sailplane up with the runway. On the way down he again uses spoilers and dive brakes to control the rate of the ship's descent.

Increased flying speed during the landing phase, after passing the pattern entry point, is a safety feature intended for extra speed to handle erratic wind conditions that may be encountered near the ground and to prevent an accidental stall at low altitudes. As the sailplane nears touchdown, the instructor flares the ship at about five feet of altitude by pulling back slightly on the stick and allowing the sailplane to settle gently onto the runway. After touchdown the ship rolls up to the flight line, brakes to a stop, and drops over on one wing. Your lesson is complete.

These procedures are repeated during the weeks that you pursue flight training. In just a few flights you'll be flying the entire landing pattern yourself, up to touchdown—at which point the instructor will take over for final contact with the ground. Your work in the air will consist of more turns, stressing coordination.

A 2-32 settles down over its own shadow on landing.

With additional straight flying you will be introduced to *straight-ahead stalls* and *turn stalls*.

As you build proficiency in your flying skills and gain confidence, your instructor will have you take over part of the flying on tow, one of the most difficult aspects of your flight training, but a skill that comes naturally in time. If you are like most beginners, you may find yourself flying on tow nearly everywhere except where you want to be: behind and slightly above the tow plane. But amazingly, when your instructor takes the controls, the ship locks in behind the tow plane as if it were on rails. In a short time you too will learn the technique and be flying the entire lesson from start to finish.

LINDA MORROW

*When you're ready for solo, your instructor signs you off with,
"Take it around the pattern by yourself."*

After you've flown alone, it's shirtcutting time on the runway.

LINDA MORROW

LINDA MORROW

"Congratulations, Pilot!"

As your flying skills and ability to set up the landing pattern develop, you realize that you're finally learning to fly. At some point, usually after thirty flights or so, your instructor will hop out and say, "OK, take it around the pattern by yourself. . . ." And though it may appear a casual decision on his part, he will allow you to fly solo only when he believes you are competent—when you demonstrate that you are ready for the responsibility—and when weather conditions are perfect.

At last the sailplane is yours alone. You take it up to release altitude, fly round the field for as long as you like or have lift, and then land again on the runway. Once down, the reaction to your solo may be a moment of private triumph marked by a grin from your instructor, or it may be a noisy celebration with a bucket of water over your head at the hands of a gang of friends. In either case your instructor will likely enact a brief ritual that dates back to the early days of aviation: He will cut the tail out of your shirt and with grease pen post on it the date of your solo and his signature. Now you can tack up the remnant on the wall of your local gliderport, along with others like it, as a souvenir of your solo flight and a symbol of your freedom in the skies!

7

WITH SAFETY IN MIND

Flying is not inherently dangerous
but, like the sea,
it is terribly unforgiving of
any carelessness or inattention

SAFETY IN FLYING is a matter of pilot attitude as much
as anything else. It requires discipline to adhere to the principles of safety taught in training, a healthy respect for the laws of
nature regarding flight and weather, and a strong sense of consideration for the rights of others.

Although we have grouped our comments about safety in one
chapter, it is not a separate topic from learning to soar. Safety
underscores every sailplane flight and lesson you will *ever* take.

SAFETY WHILE FLYING

The most dangerous situation in flying sailplanes occurs when a
pilot finds himself below pattern altitude at low speed. The risk
is that the pilot, alarmed at the nearness of the ground, will attempt a shallow turn at low speed. If excessive rudder is used,
thereby creating a skidding turn, there is a chance of stalling the

inner wing and spinning the sailplane at an altitude too low to initiate a recovery. About half of all sailplane accidents and injuries are caused by this problem.

Another contributing factor to low-altitude stalls is the *wind velocity gradient*. Under steady wind conditions the air moving close to the ground is being slowed by friction between the air and ground, and by obstacles such as bushes, trees, buildings, and variations in the natural terrain. Wind velocity increases as you move away from the ground, so that the full wind velocity occurs at a height of perhaps 100 feet. A pilot who is descending through this wind velocity gradient, while flying near stalling speed, is running the risk of having his headwind drop off enough to stall the sailplane.

All of the problems associated with low-altitude stalls and spins can be prevented by maintaining adequate airspeed at *all* times when flying the landing pattern. In the SSA training manual *The Joy of Soaring,* author Carle Conway recommends a minimum pattern airspeed of fifty percent *above* stalling speed plus one-half the estimated wind velocity.

Midair collision is a very real danger in flying—and the very thing that everyone involved in aviation works hard to prevent. To avoid this requires well-lubricated neck muscles so that you can swivel your head up and down and side to side. We can't emphasize this too strongly: *You must direct your attention outside of your sailplane cockpit.* Nothing of importance to your safety or your success as a soaring pilot is occurring inside the cockpit; you must train yourself to glance at your instruments, and return your attention to other aircraft in your vicinity, as well as the terrain below and your drift along the ground. Always look for other aircraft.

When thermaling at low speeds while banked in a tight turn, you occasionally hear a slight "burble," which indicates that an incipient stall is occurring at the wing root. This is usually of little concern. You need simply to lower the nose or flatten the bank a little, and things will be back to normal. When you are thermaling in a gaggle with other ships below, you must increase your thermaling speed slightly to avoid any possibility of having a stall develop into a spin. The thought of spinning down through a gaggle of sailplanes is enough to encourage most pilots to avoid *any* possibility of a turn stall.

PERFORMANCE LIMITATION

As we have discussed in Chapter 6: Student at the Stick, every sailplane you ever fly will have a small placard on the instrument panel giving the pilot vital information on the design and flight limitations. It is important to understand that information on this placard is not meant as recommended operating conditions, but as *absolute operating limits* that must *never* be exceeded. The placard on a sailplane gives the *maximum and the minimum weights for pilot and passenger*, if applicable, and lists the *maximum speed*, or *redline speed*—that is, the maximum speed on tow, aero, auto, or winch, and the *maximum maneuvering speed*. Maximum maneuvering speed is the highest speed at which the controls can be abruptly and fully deflected, or the highest speed at which the sailplane can be flown with safety in severe turbulence.

On the Ground

Anything on the ground—people, animals, trees, fences, buildings, cars, or other sailplanes—poses a hazard to the pilot. On landing he must be aware of the *extended float,* caused by ground effect, and stay on the runway until his speed has dropped sufficiently to be certain he can stop before he slides up behind a line of sailplanes waiting for takeoff. Bashing into someone's elegant sailplane because you didn't leave enough room to stop can be embarrassing, if not to say expensive.

LINDA MORROW

*Ground handling requires careful attention, too. These Explorers
guide a glider back to launch.*

Whenever you are visiting a gliderport, pay attention to the landing and takeoff traffic, particularly sailplanes that are landing. Sailplanes make very little noise, so if you are out on the runway and preoccupied, you may not hear them landing, and they may not see you or have enough speed or altitude to avoid you even if they do. The best rule to follow is to stay off the runways, taxiways, and the flight line unless you have some business that requires you to be there. You can see everything that is going on in safety from the sidelines.

HEALTH

Federal Aviation Administration regulations require only that the pilot be free of any known medical defect that would prevent him or her from piloting a glider. But even people in general good health should not fly if they are suffering from a cold, the flu, or any temporary malady. If you are sick, you can't devote all of your energy and attention to flying. *You should never fly if you have taken drugs.* Antihistamines, tranquilizers, and barbiturates all will adversely affect your mental alertness and reduce your ability to respond quickly and correctly to conditions encountered in flight. Amphetamines should likewise be avoided at all costs. These "pep pills" or "uppers" destroy one's judgment and are totally incompatible with flying.

Alcohol is another drug that seriously impairs a pilot's judgment and has no place in flying. Alcohol is readily absorbed into the bloodstream and, once there, interferes with the brain's function. At altitudes where only reduced amounts of oxygen are available, the effect of just a small amount of alcohol is magnified, often with disastrous results. *For these reasons FAA regulations prohibit flying within eight hours of taking a drink.*

Hypoxia, or lack of oxygen, is a serious risk when flying at high altitudes. The reduced pressure of high altitude prevents an adequate supply of oxygen from being absorbed through the lungs. Lack of oxygen, in turn, impairs the pilot's mental function. Unfortunately, the pilot may feel fine, but, much like being intoxicated, he begins to make errors. Air Force tests show that after one and a half minutes without oxygen at 25,000 feet, a pilot can no longer sign his own name. That's why responsible pilots use supplemental oxygen on every flight above 12,500 feet.

Scuba diving is a sport that, when combined with soaring, must be handled with care and understanding. *If you have been scuba diving, and especially if you have been to a sufficient depth to require decompression, you should not fly for at least twenty-four hours.* The high pressure encountered in diving dissolves excess nitrogen in your blood, and you must allow sufficient time for this excess gas to vent. Otherwise you may run the risk of suffering *an attack of the bends,* caused by a too rapid decrease in air pressure, when you are at altitude.

Safety is something that every pilot has control over and must take responsibility for. Soaring is a very disciplined sport, and the result of letting one's discipline slip can be tragic. That's why everyone involved learns and follows procedures that are designed to avoid accidents. A pilot whose attitude says, "It can't happen to me. . . . " is the one we worry about. The best and safest pilot is alert and serious and able to get his thinking far ahead of the aircraft.

8

HOW TO GET A LICENSE

THE FEDERAL AVIATION ADMINISTRATION is responsible for the regulation of all flying activities in the United States. This agency issues flying rules and regulations and establishes performance standards for pilots, instructors, and ground controllers. It also provides licensing procedures and air traffic control for the vast network of commercial flying that takes place around the country. Very little bureaucracy is apparent on the surface, however, when you begin sailplane instruction. In fact the arrangement seems quite informal. You arrive at the gliderport at the appointed time and meet with your instructor. He asks you to check out the sailplane and then assists in moving the ship from the tie-down area to the flight line. You hop in, hook up to the tow plane, and take off. What you may not realize is that the sequence you have gone through is carefully controlled by FAA regulations issued to cover flight activity. Your instructor is tested, certified, and licensed by the Federal Aviation Administration. Your glider is manufactured, maintained, and inspected according to FAA regulations. The airport operates under local and federal permits, and the traffic pattern in and around the airport is in accordance with standard procedures. So the operation and your training are far more carefully supervised than they may seem.

Just before you are ready for solo, your instructor issues you a *student license*. This permits you to fly a glider or sailplane solo or with an instructor, but you are not permitted to take up a passenger. The student license is good for a period of two years. Every ninety days you must be checked out again by a certified flight instructor with a glider rating (CFIG).

After you have flown a few hours solo, you will want to complete requirements for a *private glider pilot's license*. This rating permits you to take passengers with you and eliminates the ninety-day check flight with an instructor. However, most gliderports will either require that you have flown there within the previous ninety days or ask you to take a familiarization flight with one of their instructors. In order to get your private glider rating, you must be at least sixteen years old and show in your log book a minimum of twenty aerotow flights and a total of seven hours of solo time in a sailplane. For the private glider license you must also successfully complete the two-part FAA examination: a written and a flight test.

After you have completed the minimum flight training required by the Federal Aviation Administration, you can ask your instructor to endorse your log book, indicating that you are

LINDA MORROW

*Ground school is part of flight training, too, and a good
way to study for the FAA written exam.*

ready to take the FAA written examination. Before he will do
so, however, he will make sure that you are familiar with the
various FAA regulations that will be covered on the exam.

Concurrent with your flight training, it is important to review the soaring training manuals recommended by The Soaring
Society of America: *The Joy of Soaring* by Carle Conway and
the Society's *Soaring Flight Manual*. These two books are in-
valuable in your flight training and will provide information
necessary to take the written flight exam. The *Soaring Flight*

Manual includes a workbook and a practice examination.

When you are ready to take the FAA written examination, you may go to a local FAA office, if you live in a metropolitan area, or to a regional airport that has a designated FAA examiner on site, if you live in a rural area. You will be asked to bring along your log book with a flight instructor's endorsement, as well as positive identification in the form of a driver's license, your social security card, or a student body card. You are allowed four hours to answer the test's sixty questions, all of which are multiple choice.

The FAA examination requires your knowledge and interpretation of certain FAA regulations. To give you an idea of the test's content, listed here are a few areas it covers:

FAA regulations, Part 61, dealing with requirements for pilot certification

FAA regulations, Part 91, covering flight rules of various aircraft

Aerodynamics
Aircraft instrumentation
Weather
Aeronautical sectional charts
Planning a cross-country flight
Weight, balance, and performance data for a Schweizer 2-33
Safety
Ground handling and tow procedures

After you have completed the test and submitted it to the FAA examiner, it will be sent to the FAA central office in Oklahoma City for grading. The minimum passing score is seventy percent, and the results are valid for twenty-four months. This means that you have two years from the time you successfully complete the written test to take your in-flight examination, completing the requirements for your private glider license.

After you pass your written exam and you feel that you are ready for the flight test, it's time to go to your instructor and get a final checkout before you make a reservation with the FAA flight examiner. As part of this shakedown step, the instructor goes through a preliminary review of the requirements for flying gliders. He asks you questions about the performance of your ship and asks you to demonstrate a ground check of your glider prior to flight. Once in the air, he asks you to perform maneuvers similar to those the FAA examiner will ask of you. In effect your instructor previews your flight test. This normally requires two to three flights.

Your FAA examiner is a certified flight instructor (glider) assigned by the Federal Aviation Administration to give flight tests in your area. On the day of your exam, he gives you a brief oral quiz on the sailplane that you are about to fly and on the FAA regulations and landing patterns in use at the local field. He asks you to carry out a preflight check of the glider and to describe what you are looking for in your inspection of various connections, pins, and parts of the sailplane. Once on tow, he asks you to perform certain flight maneuvers, such as flying around the tow plane's wake, or *boxing the tow.* The objective is to move from one tow position to the other, forming a rectangular or box-like pattern, and then to return to the original position while avoiding the wake.

A flight test with an FAA-certified examiner is required to complete your private license.

When both parts of the exam are out of the way, all that remains is a handshake from your examiner and from your friends, who know you have worked hard to become a pilot. With your official private license making you a certified sailplane pilot, you can celebrate by taking a passenger up for a ride. What better way to observe your achievement and to share the joy of soaring?

9

LOOKING FOR LIFT, CROSS-COUNTRY

CROSS-COUNTRY SOARING is a matter of pitting your-self against the whimsey of nature, gambling that you can find lift and praying for a last-minute "save." It is an exercise in optimism, and one of soaring's most challenging experiences.

READY . . .

As a beginning pilot, you may be content to bore holes in the sky, delighted with your new ability and proud of any forty-five–minute flight around home field. But in time you'll increase your ability to stay up for longer periods by perfecting your thermaling techniques. Perhaps then, you'll want to try cross-country soaring, an advanced stage of the sport that takes a good deal of training and preparation. The pilot who attempts a distance task must be able to demonstrate good judgment, capable aircraft handling, and ability to fly around locally all day. He must show that he perceives changing conditions and knows how to adapt to them. He must also have the backup of a loyal crew who will track him with a trailer across the countryside and retrieve him if he lands out. Let's look at certain steps you can take as a novice pilot to ready yourself for cross-country flying.

If you run out of lift somewhere along the way and have to set it down in a convenient pasture—as inevitably happens—*it's important to be able to judge where the pasture ends and to set down before you run out of landing space.* To sharpen your skills in touching down and stopping at a predetermined point, you can work at making every routine landing on the runway count as a practice for off-field landings. Select a touchdown spot from the air and decide where you want to roll to a stop. Try to bring your ship down on the chosen spot. With repeated effort, you'll find your landing skills becoming more precise.

Another skill required is to be able to read and understand *an aircraft sectional chart.* Every area of the United States is covered by such a chart, which is reprinted every six months and can be obtained at local airports or map stores, or by writing to the Director, Coast and Geodetic Survey, U.S. Department of Commerce, Washington, D.C. 20230. Obtain the sectional chart for your local field and study it for use in planning cross-country flights. The aeronautical sectional chart represents a local area on a scale of 1:500,000 feet, or about one inch for each eight miles. It shows airports, towns, and the height of terrain in a given area. It also includes symbols for any towers or

Fig. 9-1

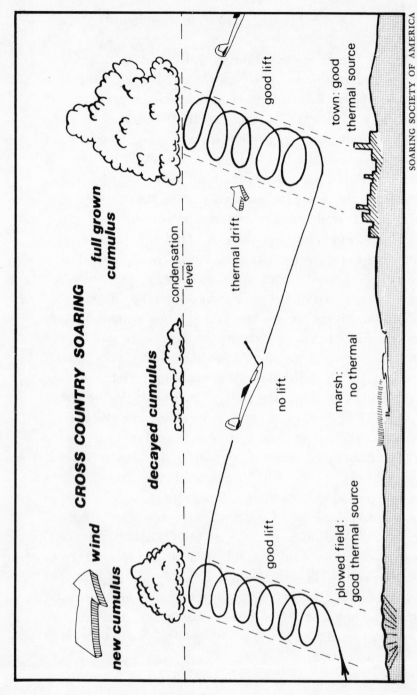

CROSS COUNTRY SOARING

wind

new cumulus

decayed cumulus

full grown cumulus

condensation level

thermal drift

no lift

good lift

good lift

plowed field: good thermal source

marsh: no thermal

town: good thermal source

SOARING SOCIETY OF AMERICA

A soaring pilot learns to find rising masses of air in which he can climb at a faster rate than the sailplane is gliding downward. When he reaches sufficient altitude he dashes off to find the next thermal.

buildings that might interfere with flight and contains navigational aids that are primarily of interest to general aviation and commercial pilots.

. . . S E T . . .

Once you feel comfortable flying solo around your gliderport and have the landing down pat, it's time to start setting tasks for yourself that take you a bit farther from home field. One way is to *plan a local flight area in the shape of an inverted cone.* It works like this. Take the L/D of your sailplane and, for good measure, divide it by two, in order to get a minimum, safe gliding angle. Add 1,000 feet to the altitude of your gliderport and consider the result your minimum pattern altitude. This is the apex of the cone. Extend the cone outward and upward at the selected glide angle to determine the safe distance that you can be away from the field and still glide back to pattern entry point. If field elevation, for example, is 1,000 feet, the pattern entry point directly above the center of the field will be at 2,000 feet. If your sailplane has an L/D of 20:1, its selected minimum glide ratio is 10 to 1. For every 500 feet of altitude, the sailplane will glide 5,000 feet, or nearly one mile. By this formula, for each additional 500 feet of elevation above pattern entry point, the sailplane can venture at least one mile farther from the field. If the altimeter reading were 3,500 feet, for example, your sailplane could be anywhere within three miles of the field and still make it back for a safe pattern entry and landing. On the local sectional chart start at the center of the field and draw concentric circles that represent the distance away from the field you are

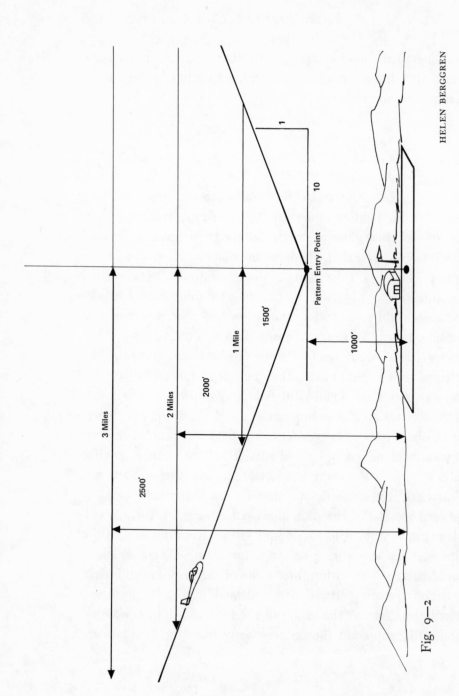

3 Miles

2 Miles

2500'

2000'

1 Mile

1500'

1000'

Pattern Entry Point

10

1

Fig. 9—2

Flying an inverted cone allows the budding cross-country pilot to begin venturing away from his home field while still being able to glide back if he doesn't find lift.

willing to be for each 500-foot increment in altitude. In our example these lines would represent one mile on the map.

When you are accustomed to flying within this inverted cone, in which you can always glide back to the gliderport, you may want to lay out a more ambitious task: a triangle slightly over three miles on a side. If the triangle is centered over the home gliderport, you will never be more than approximately two miles from the pattern entry point. Based upon our theoretical L/D of 10 to 1, you would need to maintain only an additional thousand feet of altitude above the pattern entry point to fly this ten-mile triangle. In practice you may have to adjust the position of the triangle by shifting it upwind to prevent getting caught low and downwind of the airport, and to prevent having to fight a headwind in order to get back to the field. You can make adjustments en route, as long as you pay attention to the strength of surface winds and your drift across the ground.

Now you will begin to use general aviation weather information, being alert to the forecast for the day and particularly noting temperatures aloft. Ideally, a temperature decline of 4° to 5° Fahrenheit per thousand feet of altitude is needed for a good, strong soaring day.

. . . Go

One of the first cross-country tasks for novice soaring pilots is *a Silver distance*, or a task of 50 kilometers (31.1 miles). When you're ready to try for such a goal, choose your destination and study weather patterns and wind directions. Plan your route carefully and note any alternate landing sites along the way. Plot

SCHWEIZER AIRCRAFT CORPORATI·

Flying cross-country is the soaring pilot's ultimate adventure.
This Schweizer 1–35 works his way over checkerboard terrain.

your intended course on the local sectional chart and mark off incremental distances, perhaps every five miles. Familiarize yourself with landmarks and terrain features shown on the chart so that you can quickly orient yourself while en route. Before setting off on a cross-country task, you should know techniques for determining decision altitudes. These techniques and other more detailed cross-country information are given in training manuals listed under Further Reading in this book.

After your decision to fly cross-country, you will call on all of your previous flight training and knowledge in order to fly a preselected course and find lift along the way. But if changing weather conditions look threatening, you must be ready to abandon the goal and try again another day.

On course you must pay close attention to your altitude *above ground level* (AGL). Remember, your altimeter shows your altitude *above sea level* (ASL). It's possible to be flying at a constant altimeter reading and still be getting close to the ground, because you are flying over rising terrain. When you have 3,000 or more feet of altitude AGL, you can pretty much stay on course and take lift as you encounter it. Below 3,000 feet, you must concentrate on finding lift, even if it means moving off course. At 2,000 feet AGL you must consider a potential landing site. Locate a piece of landable terrain and fly toward it, working any lift you may encounter. Check your drift over the ground to determine wind direction. Select several alternate landing sites and evaluate potential problems with each of them.

By the time you reach 1,000 feet AGL, you are committed to land. With an open field or pasture selected, you must begin to enter the landing pattern. Observe the landing area to determine wind direction and strength. Look carefully for telephone poles and wires bordering the spot. These are hard to see and can be very hazardous.

Land into the wind, if possible, unless the field is sloped. In case it is, the landing must be made uphill, regardless of wind direction. The problem here is that it doesn't take much of a slope to equal the glide angle of the sailplane. If you try to land downhill, you may never touch down, and you can run out of pasture quickly.

Many opinions circulate among soaring pilots as to the best kind of field for an outlanding. Obviously, the smoother, the better. Freshly plowed fields are nice; tall grass or corn are disastrous. But nearly everyone agrees, avoid fields with animals. A cadet at the Air Force Academy near Colorado Springs once landed out in the Academy's new Schweizer 1-26. Unfortunately, he chose a pasture that happened to have a not-so-understanding buffalo in it. Just as the ground crew arrived, so did the

STEPHEN DUPONT, COURTESY SOARING SOCIETY OF AMERICA

Who says fields don't sprout sailplanes? When this AS–W 15 landed out in a cultivated field near Bryan, Ohio, during a national contest, it attracted a crowd of onlookers from neighboring farms.

buffalo. He chased the pilot and crew back into the pickup, put a hole in the nose cone, and broke the canopy. Then he attacked the pickup! After rescuing his sailplane and returning with his crew to the gliderport, the pilot confessed to the officer in charge, "We weren't really worried about the sailplane, Sir. Just ourselves."

10

FLYING COMPETITION
AND BADGES

''THERE'S NOTHING LIKE that final glide . . . you've tried so hard and so long to get back . . . it's sometimes so exciting when you call the finish gate that you can't get the words out." These impressions of a soaring contest come from one young winner who, like other top pilots in competition, "can really put the day together and get around a task."

Big-time contest flying is a tense tournament that attracts soaring's finest pilots. The result is often a sporting battle among the clouds that covers hundreds of miles and spans one to two weeks, a contest that few spectators get to see. But if you were on the scene and able, somehow, to be several places at once, this is what you'd see. Contestants and crews, prepared to stay awhile, arrive at the meet's gliderport as long as a week in ad-

*Sailplanes line up for takeoff at national contest at
Harris Hill, New York.*

*Soaring great Paul Bikle, as competition director at a contest,
posts vital information on the task board.*

vance of the contest date. They roll onto the grounds in all manner of RVs and pull long white trailers behind them. Inside are the exquisite high-performance sailplanes they'll fly during the competition.

A soaring contest begins on the ground with a pilots' meeting, during which the weather forecast is digested and the day's task announced. A distance task of one sort or the other is usually laid out in what's called a *speed triangle*. Each pilot commits to fly around a prescribed, triangular course sometimes as long as 300 miles, photographing each turnpoint and returning to the starting line in the shortest time. It is, in effect, one, long, precision-flown cross-country sailplane race.

At the meeting contestants study task sheets, sectional charts, and well-chewed fingernails. Each ponders his chances of "winning the day," a term applied to the pilot who flies the task in the best time, earning 1,000 points and top standing for the day.

After this opening session each competitor plunges into action, much of it cerebral at first. He begins marking his navigational charts and studying weather information, trying to interpret its likely influence on his flying. He calculates and recalculates, juggling a dozen factors in his head. If he expects the day to be strong, he fills his ballast tanks with water, in order to add weight and improve the performance of his ship. He plans his strategy to get around the speed triangle and coordinates plans with his keyed-up crew. The basic idea is to determine when lift will be strongest and how much time he will take to fly the task. Then he sets a time for his flight, hopefully coinciding with optimum conditions of the day. In other words he tries to divine what the best three to four gliding hours of the day will be, a task

JOHN LEE

A contest crew washes down the ship and polishes
its surfaces for maximum performance.

tricky in itself with changing weather modifying the components of the game.

Next, the pilot prepares the cockpit. He stows maps, charts,
computers, and pencils into side pockets, along with something

to sip and to munch on. He checks parachute, oxygen equipment, and his two Instamatic cameras, mounted inside the
canopy to photograph each turnpoint when he later dips his left
wing over it. Then he runs a check of instruments, seat position,
control stick and pedals. When all is in careful order, he slips
into the cramped cockpit—accepting its confines for the next
few hours—and waits his turn to launch. When the tow plane
taxis around in front of him, he takes a tow to 2,000 feet, releases, and is free to start the contest when he chooses. He must
fly through a start gate, an invisible square window 1,000 meters
on a side, to validate his entry in the contest.

RAY MORROW

*Each sailplane is towed aloft to begin the race. If the pilot doesn't find lift
right away, he may land and try again, taking what's known as a "re-light."*

LINDA MORROW

*A contest committee scans the sky and keeps track
of competing ships by radio.*

SOARING SOCIETY OF AMERICA

*A Libelle pilot streaks over the field at over a hundred miles
per hour, dumping his water ballast in the air.*

Once on course, he must devote his attention to flying the task as fast as he can. He concentrates and assesses the sky, clouds, terrain, signs of good lift and changing weather. His focus and perception of the atmosphere around him become a serious matter. He flies in thermals, strictly for the fuel they provide him, and discards them when he's taken enough altitude. Then he's off and dashing down the course once again. What happens if he miscalculates or runs out of lift and the bottom drops out of his scheme? He picks out a harmless-looking landing space, sets down in it, and radios for a retrieve from his crew.

But if he has enough speed and altitude to finish the task, he begins his final glide, staging a dramatic moment for himself as well as for spectators on the ground. As he nears the finish gate, he swoops low to pass through it, crosses the field at a speed of over 100 mph and, only a few feet off the ground, pulls up steeply into an impressive *chandelle* around the field. After making this curving arc in the air, he lands gently on the runway.

Competing in sailplane contests takes force of mind, uncanny perception of the environment, and deft decision making. Often, the winning pilot proves to have an unflappable personality. But contest fliers and their followers are also known for their verve and sense of humor. When pilot Danny Pierson lagged behind at the 1977 U.S. Unlimited Championships and became the only contestant still not down and accounted for in the face of an approaching storm, his crew and cohorts became concerned. But then, when word came that Danny was two miles out and coming in for a finish, someone slipped a stereo cartridge of the "William Tell Overture" into the PA system. When their hero finally touched down and lifted his canopy, he heard a welcoming symphonic blast from the Lone Ranger.

When it's all over, the pilots pack up and go home, their contest becoming history. But avid followers of the sport can read a delayed account of the meet as transcribed in *Soaring* magazine. That same national contest in 1977 produced, for example, this clipped replay in that year's November issue by way of the fifth-place finisher, legendary George Moffat:

> I got to the second turnpoint as it was recycling, and had no trouble getting in or out. On the final leg, I followed a cloudstreet about 60 or 70 miles long, and gained about 1000 feet flying between 80 and 100 mph. When I reached the end of that street I jumped over to the west about 15 miles and flew another street home. It doesn't sound that exciting—flights that work well never have anything very dramatic about them. . . .

For the benefit of the would-be spectator, *Soaring* also runs a monthly calendar giving place and dates of contests being held around the country. In addition to the World Gliding Championship competition, which is held every two years for top soaring pilots around the world, soaring competition in the United States is held each year at the national and regional levels.

COMPETITION CLASSES

Open-Class ships have wingspans as long as 72 feet and have no contest restrictions as to performance-enhancing modifications.

Not surprisingly, since some of these ships have glide ratios of 50:1, the Open Class Championship is the nation's most prestigious motorless flying award. Sailplanes in the *15-Meter Class* are restricted to wingspans of not over 49.2 feet, and, generally, they have interconnecting flaps and ailerons, water ballast, and retractable landing gear as features to increase performance. *Standard Class* is similar to the 15-Meter, except that these ships are without flaps, except for those used in landing. The *1-26 Class* is the only one-design contest in the United States and is expressly for pilots of the Schweizer 1-26, a medium-performance sailplane with excellent flight characteristics. It has a 40-foot wingspan and a 21.5:1 glide ratio, and requires a particular set of flying techniques to handle well. That's how the one-design competition allows its pilots to say that "performance may be purchased, but flying skills must be earned."

The *Sports Class* is the newest competition category. It was devised to include older, lower-performance gliders as well as home-builts, transitional gliders, and others, giving them all a chance at fair competition. Contest guidelines call for handicapping the various ships according to performance, structural modifications, equipment and pilot contest experience. Since it's not realistic to expect that every young pilot can afford the cost of top-level competition, the Sports Class provides a good introduction to contest flying for the new pilot "who wants to see how the other guy does it" and to test himself against other people. Flying tasks here are not so demanding as in other classes, and a newcomer to competition might be able to fly his club's 1-26, for example, in such a contest. There's no better way to learn about competition than to fly local contests like these, which are often carried out with a country fair flavor. They often feature spot-landing contests, bomb dropping with sacks of flour, and, of course, an old-fashioned cookout. Geared to the beginning or intermediate pilot, these contests emphasize having fun with a little friendly rivalry. In soaring circles they say that you can learn more in two or three days of local contest flying than

GEORGE UVEGES

Soaring is a family affair, even if it sometimes becomes a matter of waiting for Dad to come down.

you will in weeks or months of average flying. Mike Moore helps put together such an event, the Rocky Mountain Contest, every Labor Day at Black Forest Gliderport in Colorado. He describes it as low-level competition "where twenty guys are told, 'OK, you're gonna fly fifty miles out to this place, take a turnpoint photo, fly fifty miles over there to that spot, do the same thing and come back.' On the same day one person might look at the weather and the map and say, 'I don't think I want to do this. . . . But, what the heck! Twelve other guys are goin'—I'll go.' People are more inclined to go out and get the experience they need to advance their flying skills this way."

Badges

Still another, and perhaps more obvious form of competition exists in trying to beat your own record. For those who like to keep track of their own accomplishments, The Soaring Society of America offers the *ABC Badge Program*. In simple terms levels of achievement are recognized by awarding an A pin for the first solo flight, a B pin for the first real soaring flight, and a C pin for an extended duration soaring flight. The program is administered by designated SSA instructors who are responsible for determining that requirements have been met.

The Federation Aeronautique Internationale (FAI) in Paris is the recordkeeper for all soaring achievements earned around the world. Official observers, barograph tracings, and photographs are the proof that the pilot must present, no matter where in the world he had made his flight.

The FAI Badges are internationally recognized soaring awards that begin where the ABC Badge Program leaves off. The *Silver,* *Gold,* and *Diamond Badges* require three accomplishments, or "legs," in distance, duration, and height. These, plus soarings' other proficiency badges and what it takes to earn them, are listed here:

Badge	General Requirements
A	Knowledge and understanding of FAA regulations, Parts 61 and 91
	Knowledge and understanding of preflight procedures
	Proficiency in flight maneuvers and landings required prior to solo
	First solo flight
B	Demonstration of soaring ability by solo flight *or,* thirty minutes' duration after release from 2,000-foot tow (add 1½ min/100-foot tow above 2,000 feet)
C	Knowledge and understanding of thermal, ridge, and wave soaring techniques
	Knowledge of cross-country procedure
	Two hours' minimum solo practice
	Demonstration of soaring ability by solo flight of at least 60 minutes' duration after release from 2,000-foot tow (add 1½ min/100-foot tow above 2,000 feet)
	While accompanied by an SSA instructor, demonstration of ability to a) make a simulated off-field landing approach without reference to an altimeter,

b) perform an accuracy landing from the approach, touching down and coming to a complete stop within a length of 500 feet

Silver   *Distance:* A straight line flight of at least 50 km (31.1 statute miles)
Duration: A flight of at least five hours
Height: A gain in height of at least 1,000 meters (3,281 feet)

Gold   *Distance:* A flight of at least 300 km (186.4 statute miles)
Duration: A flight of at least five hours. (The five-hour duration flight for the Silver Badge counts for the Gold.)
Height: A gain in height of at least 3,000 meters (9,842 feet)

Diamond   *Distance:* A flight of at least 500 km (310.7 statute miles)
Goal: A flight of at least 300 km over a triangular or out-and-return course (186.4 statute miles)
Height: A gain in height of at least 5,000 meters (16,404 feet)

1,000-KM Diploma   The FAI will award a special diploma to pilots achieving a distance flight of at least 1,000 km (621.4 statute miles).

In the late 1940s Robert F. Symons, a mountain pilot and wave-flying pioneer, instigated a new and unique system of awards for wave flying that he called "lennie" pins. Pilots who soar to great heights in waves receive a "one-lennie" pin for attaining an altitude of 25,000 to 35,000 feet; a "two-lennie" pin for reaching 35,000 to 40,000 feet; and a "three-lennie" pin for exceeding 40,000 feet.

Regarded as the highest soaring award in the world is the *Lilienthal Medal* of the Federation Aeronautique Internationale. It is given to reward a particularly remarkable sporting performance in gliding or eminent services over a long period of time on behalf of gliding. The award was established in 1938 in honor of Otto Lilienthal, gliding innovator and pilot. The Lilienthal Medal is made of silver and becomes the permanent property of the winner.

The Kolstad Youth Fund offers special achievement awards and a scholarship to encourage youth participation in soaring. It commemorates the late Paul K. Kolstad, an accomplished young pilot who was active in the Colorado Soaring Association. Winners of the Fund's *Century Awards* for flights of 100, 200, and 300 kilometers, respectively, receive a Century Pin and a sew-on patch. Winners of the scholarship receive a cash award ranging from $250 to $1,000 that is credited to the college of their choice. Youth of fourteen to eighteen years of age are eligible to compete for the awards, and recipients may apply for the scholarship. Interested applicants may write for detailed information to: The Kolstad Youth Scholarship Fund, 429 East San Rafael Street, Colorado Springs, CO 80903.

11

GETTING STARTED
IN SOARING

EVERYBODY CONNECTED WITH soaring would like to make it less costly if he could. But unfortunately, learning the skills of the sport is an expensive education. This reality has convinced a few young newcomers that the only way to fly is to be able to choose a rich father who has a sailplane and an instructor's rating. But if you weren't born with a control stick in your hand, don't despair. With ingenuity and motivation for becoming a glider pilot, you'll find a way to do it.

One way to get involved in soaring is to get a job at a gliderport. Working as a line boy or a line girl or clerking in the operations shack not only provides a lot of learning for a young person, it also gives him or her an income that can be applied to instruction. Certain gliderport operators pay their ground crew a modest hourly rate, and then add free flying lessons as a fringe benefit. This is what Kevin Pollock, a sophomore at Hemet High School, Hemet, California, did when his interest grew from flying radio-controlled gliders to piloting full-scale models. He got a job crewing on Sundays at Sailplane Enterprises, Inc., where he also took instruction and earned his solo rating.

Ted Everton of Ventura, California, got the kind of cooperation from his father that made his flying lessons possible. Mr. Everton agreed to drive his son ninety-five miles to the nearest gliderport and also to stake him for fifty percent of the cost of instruction. It was left to Ted to come up with $300 from part-time jobs and to keep up his flight study by reading, since he couldn't fly every weekend. He finally soloed after six months of conscientious training and patient commuting.

Amy Lockwood of Sepulveda, California, attended a summer flight school sponsored by Explorer Scouting. Her family helped her pay the cost of $325 for flying, board and room. Because she worked hard in her glider lessons as well as in the ground school, she was able to solo at the end of the two-week session, after only three hours and five minutes of flight time. She continued to enjoy soaring, driving to a commercial operation on weekends with a group of friends and renting a sailplane.

JOIN A CLUB

Soaring lends itself to group activity naturally, because you need someone on the ground to hook you to the tow plane or the winch and to run the wing tip during takeoff. After landing you also need help in retrieving your sailplane and walking its wing back to launch position. But economics too has a great deal to do with the benefits of belonging to a soaring club. Flying sailplanes is obviously not cheap recreation; necessary equipment has a cost and so does participation. The only relief for a student glider pilot is to be subsidized by an individual or a group. That's why belonging to a soaring club is the least expensive way to fly.

Nearly 200 soaring clubs operate in the United States; all are organized differently and require membership fees to join that vary from $75 to $300. Regardless of the size or the shape of the organization, a soaring club is a cooperative venture that spells relief for beginners on a tight budget. A club may be as loosely organized as six or eight people who own a glider together, or it may be more like a country club organization in which people own memberships, pay dues, and also pay a nominal fee for each flight. Monthly dues for student membership may range from $2 to $25.

If you are interested in belonging to a club, here are a few points to keep in mind. Be sure to find a club that offers instruction. Since certain organizations require that their members already hold a pilot's license before joining, it's important to search out a group of "glider guiders" that welcomes novices. The best club for a beginner will offer student rates, give away a dozen or so youth training sessions a year, or provide qualified member-instructors who will work for free. One such rare bird, said to be a member of a soaring club in Albuquerque, enjoys giving free flying lessons to the first takers who show up on Saturday mornings between 8:00 and 10:00.

Because a club is sustained by volunteer man-hours as well as cash flow, it is the perfect arrangement for a person who has more time to contribute than money. And time is what you're expected to give. Club members may find themselves running tow lines, washing sailplanes, sweeping hangars, and repairing ropes—all chores that are valuable to the club if it doesn't have to pay someone to do them. Regular members of Bay Area Soaring Associates, a club near San Francisco, have the option, for example, of paying $60 a year in dues or attending four work parties.

JIM FOREMAN

A soaring club member trades man-hours for group benefits. And washing a sailplane isn't bad duty if you get to fly it for free.

What does the soaring club member get in return? His membership dues buy him the use of club gliders, trainers, and a Schweizer 2-32, for example, and miscellaneous equipment. When the member takes a ship up, his actual flying cost may be as low as $7 per hour, one-third the commercial rate. If his monthly dues are $10 and he flies more than one hour a month, he's enjoying a bargain.

Taking advantage of a club's opportunities may cut in half the initial cost of learning to fly. A beginner might find that for $350 he can accumulate enough training and flight time to solo.

Cutting costs isn't all that a soaring club is about. Belonging to a group of soaring enthusiasts is also another way to have a good time. Mary Smothers, a globe-trotting flight instructor who lives in Iceland, feels that the greatest things about a soaring club are its atmosphere and camaraderie. She recalls, in particular, having been a member of a club in Australia where she swapped soaring stories and made lots of flying friends. "Soaring is an individual sport while you're alone in the cockpit," she said, "but after you land, it's sure nice to have people to share it with."

Many a fledgling pilot, long on enthusiasm but short on funds, has probably wished for someone to share his new-found sport with and has thought of forming a soaring club. But what may be a nearly impossible task for one young person can be accomplished by a dozen eager organizers—with the help, that is, of an established soaring club or operation. That's what a handful of line boys proved in the 1940s when they originated America's oldest and finest youth soaring group, the Juniors of Harris Hill Soaring Corporation (HHSC), Elmira, New York. These boys began flying gliders under the generous training of a TG-3 pilot and, in time, organized themselves into what became a subdivision of the senior soaring club.

Today the organization is open to youngsters aged fourteen to eighteen who pay reduced flying rates plus work-hours to belong to one of the most active and spirited groups around. A new member of the self-governing group pays $23 to join, which includes his SSA membership and a log book, and one dollar per month dues. He pays $2 for a pre-solo "instructional," plus a small rental fee for the ship. As his proficiency develops, a Junior moves from the Schweizer 2-33 to the 1-26, the Blanik, or the 1-34—all of them ships that belong to the HHSC fleet—making it possible for him to gain low-cost experience in higher-performance ships.

In exchange for student rates, Juniors help run the summer operation at historic Harris Hill, scheduling themselves to work flight line, log, and ticket sales; to work on sailplane maintenance; and to volunteer at the nearby National Soaring Museum. They also take responsibility for line operation during regional and national contests at the field, along with setting up local contests to improve flying skills of their own members. The group has sponsored many ground schools, purchased barographs and electric variometers for the senior club, begun its own soaring library, and contributed to HHSC's treasury.

But being a Junior at Harris Hill is hardly all work. One of the most popular ways to have fun is spending a few summer weeks in the cabins located on the fringe of the field. During this free-wheeling "camp," kids use any excuse—flying triumphs as well as boo-boos—to party. And being so close to the gliderport stirs its own competition to grab the best soaring conditions. "We're right there by the hangar waiting for the weather to pop into a booming day," said one Junior member. "When it happens, we're ready to race to the ships."

Because the Juniors' president, Susan Sliwa, is enthusiastic about her club and proud of its work, she encourages other young people in soaring to think of organizing themselves. "Any club or commercial organization could institute a youth soaring camp," she said. "Not only does the parent club benefit from strong and eager workers, but it's an incredible stimulus to the sport and an important character builder for young people."

. . . or Go to Camp

The idea of flight training concentrated at a summer's encampment goes all the way back to Germany in 1911. That was when university students who flew gliders began bringing other interested youth to a hill called the Wasserkuppe that was an ideal site for learning gliding. They camped together and flew together for two weeks in a kind of live-in saturation with aviation.

Today this kind of thing is carried out for teenagers by different aviation groups around the country whose two-week summer camp is a cram course in flying gliders. The flight school that Air Explorer Post Squadron 8 of Van Nuys, California, sponsors is a good example. These Explorer Scouts stage a two-week summer flight school at Edwards Air Force Base that provides flight training in both airplanes and gliders. The intent is to bring together interested teenagers from all over the United States and to give them flight training and ground school in preparation for solo and for passing the FAA written exam. Each student gets a minimum of ten hours of dual instruction, complete ground school and materials, recreational facilities, and meals

Explorer Scouts get on-field lecture in flight theory from Bill Miller.

*A. C. Woolnough diagrams the landing pattern for a student
in a moment of informal instruction.*

and lodging for two weeks for $375. The forty-odd students, a dozen of whom are in the glider program, virtually eat and sleep aviation for the period and become part of the military base near the NASA research facilities.

Coordinated by the Great Western Council of the Boy Scouts of America and hosted by the U.S. Air Force, the program also gets plenty of help from its friends: The Aircraft Owners and Pilots Association (AOPA); Cessna Aircraft, Inc.; the SSA; and Aronson's Aviation, who donates gliders and a tow plane at nearby Rosamond Airport. The program provides a strong, safe training, based entirely on volunteer instructors and counselors. A recent year's staff included a doctor, teachers, businessmen, and retired Air Force pilots—all of them certified flight instructors. They do it because they love being around people and gliders and because they want to teach safe and professional flying. The program's goal is to collect a group of young adults who share an interest in aviation, to surround them with interested adults, and to let them explore.

Head instructor Bill Miller, a former Air Force pilot and West Point graduate, explained that the "adults are here to help the kids do what they want to do." Since most of them want to solo in a glider as soon as they can, Miller lets the learning take place immediately, by giving each student time at the control stick on his or her initial flight. The idea is that the student will learn basic flight technique in the camp to the point of solo, and then progress further at his home soaring site.

Actual training at the flight school includes practice in flying tow properly; cutting loose; mastering straight stalls; turning stalls, steep turns, and landing—not to mention searching for thermals.

The Explorers' routine follows a disciplined schedule of break-fast at 6:00, flying lessons begun on the runway at 7:00, and ground school classes back at the camp in the afternoon. Then it's dinner at the base mess hall and a chapter of homework from the next day's flight syllabus. Students prepare for daily quizzes on the material and take the FAA written exam at the end of the two-week session. Despite all the hard work, they manage to fit in fun and games between learning about angle of attack and atmospheric pressure. They can see a movie at the base theater, swim at the youth center, or work out on nearby racquet ball and tennis courts. One recent summer, the Explorers were able to

LINDA MORROW

Explorer Scouts get a look at the Space Shuttle being detached from its carrier 747 at Edwards Air Force Base in California.

tour the exterior of the space shuttle Orbiter *Enterprise,* which was being de-mated from its carrier 747 at NASA's Dryden Flight Research Center. On the same tour they visited Edwards' flight line and prowled inside the cockpit of a B-1 bomber.

Teen pilots who have completed the school say that they benefited from the rapid succession of training flights and enjoyed a certain camaraderie that was a terrific experience.

Who is eligible for the program? Any Air Explorer Scout in the country from age fourteen to eighteen can apply by writing to: Air Explorer Aviation School, c/o Great Western Council/ Boy Scouts of America, P.O. Box 3198, Van Nuys, CA 91407.

Many Explorer Posts scattered around the country provide other on-going opportunities to learn to fly sailplanes, and while few are as charitable as Seattle's Post #299, where Explorers pay yearly dues of $20 and fly free, they invariably offer excellent instruction and inexpensive soaring. For a list of posts active in soaring see the directory in Chapter 13 or write to: National Director, Aviation Explorers, Boy Scouts of America, Box 61030, Dallas, TX 75261.

A similar training course in flying gliders is offered by Wave Flights, Inc., at Black Forest Gliderport outside Colorado Springs, Colorado—but in the style of a Rocky Mountain high. Black Forest's youth camp runs for four two-week sessions in June, July, and August for around $900. This program's goal too is to solo students within the two-week training, but the school also helps soloed pilots who want to learn more technique. Many campers return for a second year's session to concentrate on advanced soaring and to try their wings at cross-country.

Youth campers enjoy an informal yet cosmopolitan atmosphere that surrounds Black Forest, one of the world's most popular soaring centers, famous for its remarkable wave conditions

JIM FOREMAN

*Teenage soaring students at Black Forest, Colorado, pose alongside visiting
Paul Schweizer, co-founder of Schweizer Aircraft Corporation.*

in winter. They line up their trainers behind the tow plane
among visitors from all over the United States and Europe, all
waiting to soar over spectacular scenery along the Rockies.

Students train in gliders for six hours each day, taking turns at
crewing for each other and interspersing their flights with those
of the commercial operation nearby. They study from a profes-
sionally prepared syllabus whose lessons are designed around

*Youth campers, who crew for each other between training flights,
get ready to soar into a cloud-filled sky.*

*A flight instructor reviews a student's progress
in her log book before another lesson.*

three flights each. Other study references are *The Joy of Soaring* and FAA regulations. Ground school at the end of the day's flying is often enlivened by an afternoon thunderstorm crackling outside the combination dining room/classroom. Occasionally, class has to be delayed if the chief instructor, who is also tow pilot, must retrieve a sailplane that landed out at the end of the day. Though less formal than most classroom situations, ground school at Black Forest is a careful study plan that teaches the safest way to execute every maneuver in a sailplane, from basic control handling to emergency training. Mike Moore, Flight School Director, said, "We try to teach people how to think."

Youth campers sleep in the bunkhouse and enjoy boarding-house meals prepared for them by Mimi, the camp's cook. They relax in the evenings watching TV in the clubhouse or pile into the station wagon for a twilight ride to Pike's Peak. Other side trips might include an ice skating show at the local Broadmoor Hotel or a visit to Denver's Flight Training Center, complete with simulators and aviation exhibits. One optional session each summer offers a backpacking trip into nearby mountains. Youth campers also enjoy soaring films, horseback riding, and outdoor barbecues. One unofficial frill for the student who flies solo at youth camp is a good dousing at the hands of a gang of well-wishers from the back of a pickup truck. Word goes out when a camper is about to take his glider up alone for the first time and when he or she lands on the runway, his cohorts are waiting and whooping with a barrel of water, ready to christen the new pilot as a member of Black Forest's soaring fraternity.

Additional information on this experience is available by writing to: Black Forest Gliderport, 9990 Gliderport Rd., Colorado Springs, CO 80908; (303) 495-4144.

JIM FOREMAN

*This youth camper has just soloed, had her shirttail cut and been drenched
by well-wishers in the truck. Now she has to walk her own
wing tip back to launch.*

Only a few miles from Black Forest is the U.S. Air Force Academy, its chapel spires visible from any sailplane that flies over the area. The Academy also carries out an extensive soaring program as part of its basic aviation training, operating fifteen sailplanes and flying approximately 18,000 sorties a year. Student pilots learn to fly under Federal Aviation Regulations guidelines and receive FAA glider pilot ratings. Although the program is limited to Air Force cadets, a youngster highly motivated to get involved in soaring might consider applying to the Academy. More specific information can be had by writing to: HQ USAFA/CWOA, USAF Academy, CO 80840.

Still another entry into soaring is by way of crewing for a contest pilot. Not only does a crew member get into the excitement of a soaring contest and perform an important job, but he or she, if qualified, can often fly the pilot's sailplane at contest's end. For most young pilots it's a rare chance to fly an expensive, high-performance ship, a double bonus to the contest pilot's willingness to furnish food, shelter, teaching, and words of comfort. All that he expects in return is enthusiasm, honesty, and hard work.

12

PILOTS IN PROFILE

PART OF THE ATTRACTIVENESS of soaring is related to the people associated with the sport. Soaring enthusiasts tend to be imaginative, self-reliant, and intensely individual. They also have an enormous capacity for pleasure, which they like to express in their sport. On the following pages are sketches of ten young soaring pilots who have learned to challenge the elements and have discovered more about themselves in the process. Their accomplishments range from first solo flight to national competition, but for their early mastery of sailplanes and their clear-eyed enjoyment of the sport, we feel they're all champions.

ALAND ADAMS of Hawthorne, California, started flying sailplanes when he was thirteen. After solo he joined the Douglas Soaring Club and began to get a keener sense of the sport by being around other soaring fans and flying a variety of ships. In high

Aland Adams.

school he flew the club's Schweizer 1-26, thereby gaining more experience, and also attended a wave camp, where he learned about the wind and the rough conditions that go with wave flying.

During the summer of 1978, he had a PIK-20 at his disposal, in which he set out on a triangular cross-country flight from Rosamond Airport in the Mojave Desert, heading to a point over the White Mountains, more than one hundred miles away. Although at the beginning of the task he had to scratch along at altitudes of only 1,500 to 2,000 feet, when he eventually reached the Sierra Nevada mountain range, he was able to climb above them by running underneath the clouds and climbing to higher altitudes. After reaching his turnpoint, Aland flew cloud streets all the way back across the Owens Valley, on a seventy-mile, final glide from 18,000 feet. Comfortable with plenty of speed and altitude for his return, he was able to sit back and enjoy the sights. The task had spanned six and a half hours in the air and covered 354 miles, earning for him the distance leg of his Diamond Badge.

In a regional Sports-Class soaring contest that same year, Aland flew a PIK-20 over a speed task around a 300-kilometer triangular course, averaging 72.5 mph and setting the Junior and 15-Meter California records.

Aland and his father, Mike Adams, often go soaring in separate sailplanes, chasing around the sky and having a great time together. On one occasion, when Aland took his younger sister up as well, the three enjoyed an hour of family fun at 10,000 feet, flying along parallel and catching sight of each other from a special vantage point.

Aland feels that soaring has made him less conservative and

more independent. "I enjoy meeting the challenge of soaring head on," he said, ". . . of using my knowledge to master the elements." He is eager to fly more competition and feels it's a great way to build proficiency. "Everybody's working hard, and you gotta work even harder to get a jump ahead."

With completion of a graduate degree in mechanical engineering from Stanford University and a new job, Aland plans to purchase a high-performance sailplane and "go full bore." He also hopes to collaborate with his father, distributor for the self-launching PIK-20E, in attempting to set motorglider records.

GIL FITZHUGH lives in Basking Ridge, Pennsylvania, within driving distance of great ridge-soaring country along the Appalachian Mountains. He took his first flight at the age of twelve from the back seat of a vintage Laister-Kauffmann LK-10A, a 1943 training glider, his father at the controls. Because it was a hot day and they had lifted off the canopy beforehand, they were able to fly over the rolling green hills below them with a warm wind in their faces. But the wind also played a spooky trick on him. It set a tin plate in motion somewhere behind his seat, and the rattling sound convinced him that the rear fuselage of the glider was about to depart. Later, however, when he sat waiting on the field, the sight of his father's ship circling gracefully overhead appealed to him, and he said to himself, "I gotta do this."

Gil signed up for lessons soon after and ended up qualifying for his solo rating on his fourteenth birthday. During his first year in the air, he accumulated over fifty weekend flights, one of them giving him an altitude gain of 8,100 feet. Of his learning experience he said: "It was work, really. Except for showing you a maneuver now and then, the instructor makes you do the whole thing. You're working and sweating the whole time. Back

RAY MORROW

Gil Fitzhugh.

on the ground he tells you what you did wrong, and sometimes you're not sure you're progressing . . . but then it starts to get easier . . . and takeoffs and landings are fun."

After soloing Gil went out to Ridge Soaring Gliderport and took further training in approaches with famous pilot and instructor Tom Knauff. During a subsequent flight, he found himself soaring in formation over Bald Eagle Ridge, by chance with world out-and-return record holder, Karl Striedieck.

Since then, Gil has been checked out to fly the LK-10, its wings recovered in the original Army markings, as well as the Schweizer 2-23 and 1-26. He is eager to develop his flying skills and has drawn his best friend into the sport; the two of them work odd jobs after junior high classes to pay for soaring lessons. Because he likes mathematics and flying so much, he figured "there's bound to be a career in there somewhere."

ALISON GLASS, who lives in Newport Beach, California, first learned about flying sailplanes by way of *Soaring* magazine, where she saw an ad for summer camp in Colorado. Learning another sport that would put her outdoors in the open interested her; she was already a competitive sailor. So she went to Black Forest's two-week youth soaring camp, where she quickly became an enthusiast on her demo ride. Afterward, her instructor remarked that having Alison in the front seat of a trainer was "like flying with a cheerleader." On a later training flight she circled under an enormous cumulus cloud and got a real view of its fleecy arched cavity in the center. "It was beautiful," Alison remembered. ". . . one of those moments that stays with you forever."

The practical side of Alison's experience at youth camp wasn't quite so inspiring. She had so little luck finding lift and staying up that her friends and instructors tagged her "The Streamlined Rock." At the session's caboose party they presented her with a "Black Forest Sky Hook" designed for attaching to the clouds. On returning to California, however, and flying at Elsinore, she had a day's soaring that reversed her image. On her first solo flight there, she went up in a Schweizer 2-33 and stayed aloft for two and a half hours, gaining 5,000 feet and having the time

Alison Glass.

of her life. At one point while thermaling over the hills below, she looked out of the canopy to see a hawk who had flown up beside her to climb in the same air current. He flew with her for a few seconds in that rare bond between sailplane pilot and bird, and then soared off in another direction.

Alison feels that soaring has made her more independent because it calls on her decision-making skills and demands so much of her concentration. She plans to attend a ground school course at a local junior college in preparation for her private pilot's license and looks forward to being able to take her friends flying. Later she wants to train for cross-country by working on thermaling and weather-watching, both of which are efforts designed to sharpen her skills for competition as well. Eventually, she hopes to learn aerobatics, having found that spins and wing-overs are exciting. She said, "Looking straight down, with the wings rotating around you . . . wow! It's great, and I've never really been frightened."

GALEN FISHER is part of the teaching staff at Sailplane Enterprises, Inc., Hemet, California. He became interested in airplanes in junior high school and initially took lessons in a power plane. But after he sampled gliding and discovered that he could get a glider license as early as his fourteenth birthday, he switched. After soloing, he was lucky enough to log a number of hours in a Schweizer 1-34, refining his skills and becoming very comfortable at the controls. Then, when he reached the age of sixteen, he applied his knowledge of gliding to power instruction and earned his pilot's license without difficulty. He earned his rating as a Certified Flight Instructor in Glider at twenty and gave lessons at a gliding club organized at the University of Califor-

RAY MORROW

Galen Fisher.

nia at San Diego, where he was a student. This gave him even more chances to fly and to enjoy the social benefits of a club. "Clubs are really nice," he said. "You can go out on a weekend and have fun with people who have the same interest as you." He also pointed out that clubs take the edge off an expensive sport.

Galen holds his Silver Badge and his Gold altitude leg, which he achieved by soaring in thermal conditions under clouds near Hemet. He reached 13,000 feet at one point, which satisfied the 3,000-meter gain above release point. He said he's looking forward to his Gold Badge cross-country attempt, which he will aim for with a 300-kilometer flight from Hemet to the Mexican border. He looks forward to this task as a mental challenge that he has to prepare himself for. "Because," he said, "it's things inside you that block you from making it. It's not a matter of conditions not being good enough."

Galen has bought a hang glider in order to diversify and will set about learning to fly it.

Eric Rosenquist of Vail, Colorado, began flying sailplanes at the age of eighteen, when he was a freshman at Colorado College and found himself invitingly close to Black Forest Gliderport. He enjoys being able to relax from working and studying by soaring along the Rockies near Colorado Springs in his PIK-20. Although he appreciates the potential of his high-performance ship and has earned the altitude leg of his Silver Badge, he said he's "not too concerned with chasing badges." Instead, like so many other pilots, he enjoys the idea of testing his own competence in a sailplane. As he put it, "Soaring is such a gut-level thing. . . . It's survival in terms of staying up, and you

JIM FOREMAN

Eric Rosenquist.

have to be tenacious."

On one of his favorite forays aloft, however, he got into strong lift that required very little tenacity of him. "I was in the PIK," he recalled, "at 14,000 feet below a cloud, with lift all around. I was flying through the low-hanging wisps of clouds that were like gates in a slalom ski race. The neat thing was not having to look for lift but just making sure I was flying fast enough so that I wouldn't get sucked into the clouds."

Eric clearly takes great pleasure in his sport and likes what it does for him. "It really strokes my ego to do well in soaring," he said. "It restores my beleaguered sense of individuality."

SCOTT IMLAY took a few glider lessons when he was in the eighth grade, during a visit to Estrella Sailport in Arizona. After several flights with prominent pilot/instructor Les Horvath, Scott was hooked. When he returned home to Seattle, Washington, where he still lives, he completed his training as a member of Aviation Explorer Post #299.

One of his most memorable flights occurred after he had gone to Bald Eagle Ridge, Pennsylvania, at the invitation of local gliderport proprietor Tom Knauff. The day after Scott arrived turned out to be a spectacular soaring day, so he rented a Schweizer 1-26 and set out over a triangular course. But ridge soaring proved to be quite a different experience for him; he recalled: "When you're thermal flying, you're up high and you have time to relax and prepare yourself for maneuvers. But on the ridge you just have to take things as they come and really stay alert. I was down near ridge height most of the time—about 800 to 2,500 feet above the valley floor—and there weren't that many places to land. I got into lots of turbulence, and it was tricky . . . but I really enjoyed that flight." It carried two other rewards as well: the distance leg of Scott's Gold Badge and the goal requirement for his Diamond Badge.

Scott, who is an aeronautical engineering student at the University of Washington and a weekend flight instructor at nearby Soaring Unlimited, also flies power. But he would much rather fly a glider for the challenge it presents. "Power flying is mostly procedures," he explained. "A glider is very dynamic. . . . You're free, and everything is changing by the moment. Using what's there—in nature—rather than creating your own means of propulsion, has to be exciting."

Scott became interested in competition very early in his soaring career, having been influenced by the teaching orientation of Horvath as well as being lucky enough to have access to a Schweizer 1-26 that he could fly to practice cross-country technique. It paid off. In 1978, with the support of his family who crewed for him, Scott flew in the U.S. National 1-26 Championships held in Hobbs, New Mexico. After five days of hot competition against the country's top 1-26 pilots, nineteen-year-old Scott won the meet. One of his fellow contenders, Frank Connor, later wrote in *Soaring* magazine:

> Our champion, Scott Imlay, is a rather shy, very friendly young man. . . . His victory should provide inspiration to all the younger pilots, and we shall look forward to hearing his name many times in the future. I shudder to think of competing against him as he gets even better. . . .

Scott, for his part, can hardly wait. He wants to get into other competition aircraft and to train for national and international

Scott Imlay.

contests. His advice for beginning pilots who want to learn cross-country flying? "Don't get discouraged; keep trying! Sooner or later, it'll work out for you."

ALICE GOODLETTE of Littleton, Colorado, grew up around soaring under the influence of her father who also is a sailplane pilot. Starting out with a three-lesson mini-course when she was fifteen, she soloed at the end of her first summer of training and earned her B and C Badges, plus her private pilot's license (glider) within the next year. She has since passed her Commercial Glider Pilot flight test, which allows her to earn money giving glider rides and serves as a stepping stone to becoming an instructor.

On the final day of a local Labor Day soaring contest she had entered at Black Forest, Alice hooked up to a series of strong thermals, including one boomer that she rode to 13,000 feet. After nearly four hours she found herself one hundred miles downwind of the gliderport, but out of lift. By this time she was low on altitude, so she picked out a gently rolling open pasture and set down her Schweizer 1-26, ending the longest flight of her life. When asked how she regarded the potential hazards of cross-country soaring, she said, "There's really no problem getting the sailplane down safely as long as you know the countryside."

Alice also attended a series of high-altitude training sessions in preparation for an eventual wave flight. One day during her senior year in high school, the wave was working, and Alice got ready. She arranged for the necessary oxygen equipment, gave her ship a thorough preflight check, then bundled up in warm clothing and took off. On tow she encountered severe rotor turbulence. In an instant her sailplane would seem to drop out from under her, thrusting her up against her shoulder straps and belt, then slam her back into her seat. With wing spars creaking and groaning, it took all of Alice's concentration and pilot skill

Alice Goodlette.

to maintain her position on tow. But as suddenly as the turbulence started, it stopped. Her variometer indicated lift, increasing rapidly from 100 to 500 feet per minute (fpm). Alice released, turned into the wind, and began to penetrate into the wave. As she moved into the mainstream of the invisible fountain of air flowing upward, she entered a silent world of eerie calm. There was no sensation of movement, no sound, save the gentle rush of air over the wings. It was a world away from the violent gyrations of a moment earlier. As lift increased, she picked out visual references on the ground in order to maintain position in the wave. After half an hour, she had reached 25,000 feet. She was still climbing, but now at a slower rate. Outside, the air temperature registered 30° below zero. Her breath was beginning to condense on the inside of the canopy, limiting visibility. She looked down at the magnificent view of the Continental Divide and decided the rough ride had been worth it. As she sat in the cold cockpit, concentrating on her position and airspeed, she watched the lift steadily decline. Finally, in zero lift at 29,900 feet—Pike's Peak tucked under her left wing nearly two and a half miles below—Alice opened her spoilers. She pushed the nose of her sailplane down and began the long descent to the gliderport below.

How had she felt, alone in the quiet world of the wave? "Cold," she remembered, "but really happy." Realizing that she now qualified for a "one-lennie" pin must have warmed her heart.

FRED VOLTZ soars over the scenic lake country and checkerboard fields that extend from the area outside Milwaukee, Wisconsin. He first took flight training at the age of twelve from his

Fred Voltz.

father, Gunter Voltz, an instructor and soaring devotee. Fred soloed in a glider at the age of fourteen and in a power plane on his sixteenth birthday. An active member of Thermal Sniffers Soaring Club, he is working on a commercial license and an instrument rating that will take him closer to his career goal of becoming an airline pilot and allow him, in the meantime, to work as a flight instructor. He has earned the Century I and II Awards for 100- and 200-kilometer flights, respectively, and has won the Kolstad Scholarship for $500. Fred holds the Silver Badge and the altitude leg of his Diamond Badge, which he earned with a flight over Colorado while on a soaring vacation there. He has also been accepted to the Air Force Academy.

Fred's most memorable soaring experience took place while he was still a novice cross-country pilot. He flew an RK-7 on a straight downwind dash of over 137 miles into Illinois before he landed out in a farmer's newly harvested pea field. Members of the farmer's big family greeted him as if he were a celebrity, helped him disassemble his ship, and invited him in for dinner. Fred claims there's no better way to make friends.

He believes that it pays a young pilot to stick with soaring and claim the sense of accomplishment that comes with experience. "After you get a few cross-country flights," he said, "you begin to feel that soaring's more than going up and gliding down . . . that this is a *real* sport."

Tom Frazer of Santa Rosa, California, flies sailplanes out of Calistoga Soaring Center. Since both his mother and father fly power, he has grown up around airplanes. He joined the SSA at the age of thirteen, mainly so that he could receive *Soaring* magazine and get a feel for the sport by reading about it. He at-

LINDA MORRO

Tom Frazer.

tended soaring youth camp in Colorado the summer he was fourteen, being particularly interested in the back-to-basics aviation training he felt he could get only in a glider program. While there, he flew his first solo, taking along a barograph in order to have its trace as a memento. And a memorable solo it was! After releasing from tow, Tom picked up lift in a small thermal and hopscotched his way to other thermals with stronger lift, finally taking one all the way to cloud base and over the 1,000-meter gain in altitude leg required for the Silver Badge. By the time he landed, he had also completed requirements for his A, B, and C Badges.

Tom appreciates the sense of achievement he gets in a sailplane. "Although flying a trainer is like driving a truck, really," he said, "once you land and know you've pulled off a good flight, it's a great feeling of accomplishment." He also articulated the sport's esthetic appeal to him. "From the cockpit of a sailplane, the earth takes on a beauty that never becomes commonplace."

On one flight in particular, when Tom had advanced to a Schweizer 1-34, he felt a connection with nature that was very special: "I got up to cloud base by blundering into thermals and staying magically out of sink. As I began dipping and turning my ship in the diffused grey light, I put on a tape and the headphones to my cassette player. Rain began pelting the canopy gently, with a flash of lightning off my wing every now and then accompanied by a boom of thunder that would make the ship vibrate. The music fit the mood perfectly—grey and introspective, but with a sense of urgency. During those minutes, the weather and the sailplane were tied together by the music. It was one flight I'll never forget."

LINDA MORRO

Kevin Wayt.

KEVIN WAYT lives in Santa Ana, California. He built and flew radio-controlled gliders in grade school, before getting involved in flying himself. After training with his father, a retired airline pilot and certified flight instructor, Kevin soloed in a sailplane at the age of fourteen. His first cross-country adventure resulted in a five and a half hour flight of 165 miles that took him from El Mirage, California, to Las Vegas, Nevada. But much to his frustration, he discovered at flight's end that the barograph on board had not been operating to make the feat official. So he chalked it up to experience and tried again. He eventually earned his Diamond distance and goal legs, back to back, and on one special day when he was flying over Elsinore, California, he ran into 1,000-fpm lift that took him to 20,000 feet, allowing him to satisfy his altitude gain requirement and to complete his Diamond Badge. He was seventeen at the time.

When Kevin and his dad acquired a new sailplane, a high-performance Standard Cirrus, he got the chance to fly with water ballast for the first time, and later came in second at a regional contest at El Mirage. At the 1975 Nationals he placed twentieth in a field of sixty contestants, despite a couple of bad days when he had to land out.

With the benefit of his father's expertise and encouragement, Kevin said, "I've been very fortunate . . . and I really never studied a lot; I just sorta got in and went. Flying competition is really an extension of cross-country soaring and makes a better pilot of you," he explained, "because you gotta push and take the chance . . . and you get to gauge yourself against people who've been doing it a long time."

Kevin obviously relishes the demands of competition, but he also loves the reflective aspect of soaring. "Sometimes I'll soar to get away from the city and smog. . . . I'll try and 'climb' a mountain peak like San Jacinto. And I really can't tell you what a sensation it is to soar quietly past hikers who, like myself, have gotten to the top!"

13

WHERE TO SOAR IN THE USA

*Following is a condensed listing from the
1980 Directory of Soaring Sites and Organizations, by permission of The Soaring
Society of America.*

ALABAMA   No soaring sites currently operating in this state.

ALASKA   *Alaska Soaring Association, Bradley Field, southeast of
Fairbanks, near town of North Pole (c/o Marvin W. Falk, 174
Hamilton Way, Fairbanks 99701); (907) 479-3587.

ARIZONA   *Arizona Soaring Association, Estrella Sailport and Turf
Soaring (PO Box 11214, Phoenix 85061); (602) 949-0838.

Arizona Soaring, Inc., Estrella Sailport, 20 miles south-south-
west of Phoenix, I-10E, Exit 162A (PO Box 27427, Tempe 85282);
(602) 568-2318.

*Tucson Soaring Club, Ryan Field, 12 miles west of Tucson
85717; (602) 883-9913.

Turf Soaring School, Pleasant Valley Airport, 15 miles northwest of Phoenix, 8902 West Carefree Hwy. (PO Box 1586, Black
Canyon Stage, Phoenix 95029); (602) 582-3621.

* Starred sites are soaring clubs.

ARKANSAS   Southern Soaring, Inc., Finley Gliderport, 4 miles east
of Marion (PO Box 330, Marion 72634); (501) 735-8811 or
735-2449.

CALIFORNIA (NORTHERN)
    *Aero Pines, Brownsville, 130 miles northeast of San Fran-
cisco, 80 miles north of Sacramento, 80 miles west of Reno (c/o
Bill Rodenburg, Brownsville Airport 95919); (916) 675-2321.
    *Ames Soaring Club, Hummingbird Haven, Hwy. 580 to Green-
ville Rd., south to Patterson Pass Rd. (8638 Patterson Pass Rd.,
Livermore 94550); (415) 447-4110 or 376-6373.
    *Bay Area Soaring Association, Skysailing (Fremont), behind
drag strip on west side of State Hwy. 17 at Durham Blvd. offramp
(2728 Oak Rd., #146, Walnut Creek 94596); (415) 356-9576 or
984-3045.
    Big Valley Soaring, Kingdon Airpark, Hwy. 5 to Hwy. 12, south
to Thornton Rd., south to De Vries (12145 De Vries Rd., Lodi
95240); (209) 466-9820 or 943-0908.
    Calistoga Soaring Center (1546 Lincoln Ave., Calistoga 94515);
(707) 942-5592.
    *Chico Soaring Association, Inc., Chico Municipal Airport,
north of city (PO Box 1571, Chico 95927); (916) 342-6559.
    Donner Aviation, Inc., east side of Truckee Airport, 2½ miles
east of Truckee, Hwy. 267 (PO Box 2657, Truckee 95734); (916)
587-6702.
    *East Bay Soaring Club, Inc., Calistoga (441 San Carlos Way,
Novato 94947); (415) 897-4792.
    *North Bay Soaring Association, Sonoma Skypark, 3 miles
southeast of Sonoma (19 Farm Rd., San Rafael 94901); (415)
472-1274.
    *Northern California Soaring Association, Hummingbird Haven
Airport, 4 miles east of Livermore (PO Box 338, Livermore
94550); (415) 447-4110.
    *Sacramento Soaring Club, Inc., Hwy. 80 to Truckee, south to
airport (7157 Sunset Ave., Fair Oaks 95628); (916) 961-8854.
    Sky Sailing Airport, Durham Rd. exit off Hwy. 17, left on
Christy St. (44999 Christy St., Fremont 94538); (415) 651-7671
or 656-9900.

*Soaring Experience, Inc., Sky Sailing Airport, Durham Rd. off Hwy. 17, south on Christy St. (PO Box 2547, Airport Station, Oakland 94614); (415) 529-6404.

Vacaville Soaring, Inc., Vacaville Gliderport, between Fairfield and Vacaville on Hwy. 80 (PO Box 176, Vacaville 95688); (707) 448-4610.

CALIFORNIA (SOUTHERN)

*Academic Soaring Club, Hemet-Ryan Airport, 2 miles west of Hemet (2100 Cahuilla, Colton); (714) 824-3628.

*Antelope Valley Soaring Club, El Mirage Airport (El Mirage Airport, RR 1, Adelanto); (805) 942-0786.

Aquarian Soaring, Lone Pine Airport (north of Los Angeles 214 miles on Hwy. 395) (PO Box 920, Lone Pine 93545); (714) 876-5756.

Aronson's Air Service, Rosamond Airport, Hwy. 14 to Rosamond, 11 miles north of Lancaster (PO Box J, Rosamond 93560); (805) 256-2200 or 948-9016.

*Associated Glider Clubs of Southern California, Ltd., Skylark Field and Jacumba (PO Box 3301, San Diego 92103); (714) 449-5888.

Borderland Air Sports Center, 9 miles northeast on Hwy. 805 to Otay Lakes Rd., Telegraph Canyon Rd. Exit (4627 Vista St., San Diego 92116); (714) 421-9292 or 283-8915.

*Cumulo Nimbus Escadrille, Inc., AF Reserve Air Station, Los Alamitos (c/o Garnet G. Sandeen, LTC, 2718 Sandpiper Dr., Costa Mesa 92626); (714) 546-1357.

*Cypress Soaring, Inc., Hemet-Ryan Airport, west of town on Hwy. 74 (PO Box 694, Cypress 90630); (714) 687-0289.

*Douglas Soaring Club, El Mirage Field, west of Adelanto (summer), Skylark Gliderport at Lake Elsinore and Rosamond (winter) (5224 Rockland Ave., Los Angeles 90041); (213) 255-8691 or 869-4067.

*Elsinore Valley Soaring Club, Skylark Field, Elsinore (1950 Midwick, Altadena 91001); (213) 798-2388.

Great Western Soaring School, Crystalaire Airport, 4 miles east of Pearblossom on Hwy. 138, turn south on 165th St. E, 1½ mi. (PO Box 189, Pearblossom 93553); (805) 944-2920.

*Glider Division Navy Aero Club, Armed Forces Reserve Center, Los Alamitos AS (39 Nieto Ave., Long Beach 90803); (213) 438-8818.

*Mount Whitney Soaring, Inc., Lone Pine Airport (PO Box 775, Lone Pine 93545); (714) 876-4590.

*Orange County Soaring Association, Perris Valley Airport, south of Perris, west of Hwy. 395 (PO Box 5475, Buena Park 90620); (714) 522-6015.

Sailplane Enterprises, Hemet-Ryan Field, west of Hemet, south of Hwy. 74 (PO Box 1650, Hemet 92343); (714) 658-6577.

Sierra Soaring, Inyokern Airport, 1 mile west of Inyokern (PO Box 601, Inyokern 93527); (714) 375-4281.

Skylark Gliderport at El Mirage Sky Ranch, 12 miles west of Adelanto on El Mirage Rd. (Star Route, PO Box 102, Adelanto 92301); (714) 388-4374.

Skylark North, Fantasy Haven Airport, Tehachapi, Highline Rd., 2½ miles southeast of town (PO Box 918, Tehachapi 93561); (805) 822-5267.

*Southern California Competition Club (c/o Gerald E. Giddens, 714 S Glendale Ave., Glendale 91205); (213) 245-6861. (Set up to teach competition organization and encourage competition flying.)

*Southern California Soaring Association Flight Group, El Mirage (c/o Von Ross, 260 St. Albains Ave., South Pasadena 91030); (213) 255-7815.

Steck Aviation, Inc., Brown Field, south on I-5 or I-805 to State Rt. 117, east to airport (Bldg. 2053, Brown Field, San Diego 92173); (714) 425-0570 or 427-9741.

Super Cub Services, California City Municipal Airport (20036 Airway Blvd., California City 93505); (714) 373-4118.

*29 Palms Soaring Club, 29 Palms Airport, 10 miles west of 29 Palms (PO Box P-891, 29 Palms 92277); (714) 367-3186.

*UCSD Soaring Club, Torrey Pines Gliderport, Elsinore, Jucumba (PO Box B-023, La Jolla 92093). (Offers instruction/pleasure flying to students, staff, faculty, and alumni of UCSD.)

COLORADO   *Colorado Soaring Association, Black Forest Gliderport, 7 miles northeast of Colorado Springs on south edge of Black Forest (9990 Gliderport Rd., Colorado Springs 80908); (303) 495-4144.

Gliders of Aspen, Aspen Airport, 6 miles northwest of Aspen, Hwy. 82 (PO Box 175, Aspen 81611); (303) 925-3418 or 925-3694.

*High Flights Soaring Club, Meadow Lake Airport, 10 miles northeast of Colorado Springs, Hwy. 24 (380 Goldcamp Rd., Colorado Springs 80906); (303) 634-0387 or 576-1343.

Soaring Society of Boulder, Boulder Municipal Airport, northeast of Boulder off Valmont Rd. (PO Box 1031, Boulder 80306); (303) 499-2190.

The Cloud Base, Inc., Boulder Municipal Airport, north on US 36 to CO 119E (Longmont Diagonal), 1 mile to Rt., turn east on Independent Rd., 6/10 mile (Airport Rd., Boulder 80301); (303) 530-2208 or 530-3110.

*USAF Academy Soaring Club, USAF Academy Airstrip (CWOA Soaring, USAF Academy 80840); (303) 472-2620.

Wave Flights, Inc., Black Forest Gliderport (9990 Gliderport Rd., Colorado Springs 80908); (303) 495-4144 or 495-2436.

Waverly West Soaring Ranch, 15 miles north of Fort Collins off I-25 (PO Box 1055, Fort Collins 80522); (303) 568-3374.

Western Flight Training, Inc., Boulder Municipal Airport, northeast of Boulder on Valmont (Municipal Airport, Boulder 80301); (303) 444-2041.

CONNECTICUT

Connecticut Cu-Climbers Soaring Group, Inc., Chester Airport, Exit 6 off CT 9, 3 miles west (34 Fernwood Grove Rd., Old Saybrook 06475); (203) 388-3295.

Connecticut Soaring Center, Waterbury Gliderport, 6 miles north of Waterbury on Rt. 262 (South Street, Plymouth 06782); (203) 283-5474.

*Connecticut Yankee Soaring Club, Canaan Airport Canaan, 1 mile northwest of town (Loren C. Caddell, 34 Catonah St., Ridgefield 06877); (203) 438-4324.

*Nutmeg Soaring Association, Inc., Canaan Airport, Rt. 44 to Main St., 1 mile northeast (c/o Charles A. Skelton, 19 Milwood Dr., Branford 06405); (203) 488-9770.

*Tunxis Soaring Club, Canaan, 1 mile northwest of Center (40 Vantana Dr., Bristol 06010); (203) 582-8530.

DELAWARE   No soaring sites currently operating in this state.

FLORIDA   *Apalachee Soaring Society, Quincy Airport, 1 mile northeast of Quincy on FL 12 (2248 Trecott Dr., Tallahassee 32308); (904) 385-4627 or 575-4767.

*Central Florida Soaring Club, Willis Gliderport (Rt. 1, Box 1100X, Boynton Beach 33437); (305) 737-8799.

Citrus Soaring, Maguire Airport, 10 miles west of Orlando off Hwy. 50 on Rt. 439 (PO Box 86, Olee 32761); (305) 656-9860.

*Coastal Aviation, Inc., Coastal Airport, Alternate 90W to Pensacola (Rt. 8, PO Box 626, Pensacola 32506); (904) 944-0620 or 944-0621.

Glades Soaring School, Kendall Gliderport, 168th St., SW 237th Ave., 9 miles west of Krome Ave., US-27, west at 192nd St. SW (PO Box 970664, Miami 33197); (305) 232-2700.

Lenox Flight School, Arcadia Municipal Airport, Hwy. 70E to Airport Rd. (Rt. 4, PO Box 4639, Arcadia 33821); (813) 494-3921.

*North Florida Soaring Society, Herlong Airport, Normandy Blvd., 3 miles west of I-295 (7853 La Sierra Ct., Jacksonville 32216); (904) 264-8444.

Rudy's Gliderport, 20 miles northwest of Gainesville (Rt. 1, PO Box 102, High Springs 32643); (904) 454-1312.

SAIL PLANES INC., Herlong Field, 3 miles west of I-295 on Normandy Blvd. (1441 University Blvd. N, Jacksonville 32211); (904) 743-1944 or 724-4655.

Sebring Soaring Centre, Inc., Sebring Airport, 98 off US 27 or 17 from center of Sebring (Bldg. 100, Rt. 2, PO Box 552, Sebring Airport, Sebring 33870); (813) 655-2397.

Sky Sailors Association, Inc., 1646 Pasadena Drive, Dunedin 33528; (813) 733-5132.

Soaring Seminoles, Inc., Flying Seminoles Ranch, 3 miles east of Oviedo on Hwy. 419 (Rt. 1, PO Box 475, Oviedo 32765); (305) 365-3201.

*Suncoast Soaring Association, Hibiscus Airport, 6 miles west of Vero Beach on Rt. 60 (826 17th Ave., Vero Beach 32960); (305) 562-6910.

*The Soaring School, Circle T Ranch Airport, 33 miles northeast of West Palm Beach (PO Box 566, Indian Town 33456); (305) 597-3228.

Winter Haven Soaring, Gilbert Field, Winter Haven (US Hwy. 92, 11716 Fife Ave., Tampa 33617); (813) 956-3765.

GEORGIA *GLERC (Georgia Lockheed Employees Recreational Club), Monroe Soaring Association, Rt. 78 east to Monroe (86 South Cobb Dr., Marietta 30061); (404) 971-8039 or 424-2938.

*Mid-Georgia Soaring Association, Monroe Municipal Airport, southeast border of Monroe (PO Box W, Monroe 30655); (404) 267-5686.

Peach State Gliderport, Williamson, 35 miles south of Atlanta, 6 miles west of Griffin Hwy. 362 (PO Box 52, Williamson 30292); (404) 227-8282.

*Sea Islands Soaring Society, Inc., Plantation Air Park, 8 miles south of Sylvania on Hwy. 21 (PO Box 13919, Savannah 31401); (912) 355-6938.

HAWAII Honolulu Soaring Club, Inc., Dillingham Airfield, 6 miles west of Waialua (PO Box 626, Waialua 96791); (808) 623-6711.

Oahu Soaring Club, Inc., Dillingham Airfield, Mokulei, 25 miles west of Honolulu (PO Box 629, Hauula 96717); (808) 293-9348.

IDAHO Condor Sky Sailing, Inc., Hailey Airport, Hwy. 75 (PO Box 1101, Hailey 83333); (208) 788-3054.

Inland Empire Soaring Council, Sandpoint City-County Airport (PO Box 187, Sagle 83860).

Red Baron Soaring, Teton Peaks Airport, adjacent to Driggs (Teton Peaks Airport, Driggs 83422); (208) 354-8131 or (307) 353-2703.

*Teton Valley Soaring Club, Teton Peaks Airport, Driggs 83422; (208) 354-8131. (Social club using Red Baron facilities.)

ILLINOIS Air Display, Inc., Park Forest South, ½ mile south of Sank

Trail on Rt. 54 (1029 Wingate Rd., Olympia Fields 60461); (312) 748-2102 or 747-0353.

*Chicago Glider Club, Chicago Glider Club Field, Rt. 2 (PO Box 618E, Minooka 60447); (815) 467-9861.

*Chicago Glider Council (Wm. Carlson, 324 Harlem Ave., Glenview 60025); (312) 724-8436.

*Decatur-Moweaqua, Decatur, 5 miles east of Decatur and Moweaqua, 10 miles south of Decatur, 1 mile north of Rt. 51 (4356 Leonore Dr., Decatur 62526); (217) 877-1395.

Hinckley Soaring, Inc., Hinckley Airport, 2 miles west of Hinckley on US 30 (Hinckley Airport, Hinckley 60520); (815) 286-7200.

*Northern Illinois Glider Club, Clow Airport, Plainfield, southwest corner of Boughton and Naperville Rds. (c/o 835 Curtiss St., Apt. 202, Downers Grove 60515); (312) 969-8261 or 455-7739.

*Northern Illinois Soaring Association, Freeport "Alburtus" Airport, 3 miles south-southeast of Freeport, 35 miles west of Rockford, 110 miles west-northwest of Chicago (4455 E Charles St., Apt. 314, Rockford 61108); (815) 226-9298.

*Soarheads, Inc., Clow International Airport, 2 miles west Bollingbrook on Boughton Rd. (c/o 1874 Carriage Hill Rd., Lisle 60532); (815) 420-0753.

*Wabash Valley Soaring Association, Inc., Lawrenceville-Vincennes Municipal Airport, 5 miles northeast of Lawrenceville (PO Box 287, Lawrenceville 62439); (618) 943-2076.

Windy City Soaring Ltd., Clow International Airport, off Naperville Rd. in Plainfield (Rt. 2, PO Box 201C, Plainfield 60544); (312) 759-2046.

INDIANA Callahan Aviation, Inc., Kendallville Airport, 1½ miles north of Kendallville on Hwy. 3 (RR 3, Kendallville 46755); (219) 347-1066.

*Central Indiana Soaring Society, Terry Airport, 20 miles northwest of Indianapolis on Indiana Hwy. 32 (Indianapolis Terry Airport, Zionsville 46077); (317) 359-9714.

*Lafayette Soaring Society (1145 Rochelle Dr., Lafayette 47905); (317) 463-1266.

IOWA *Burlington Soaring Association, Inc., Burlington, 1 mile southwest of town (16 Cascade Terrace, Burlington 52601); (319) 752-8789.

*Central Iowa Soaring Society, Inc., Perry, 1 mile west of city (935 Insurance Exchange Bldg., Des Moines 50309); (515) 288-1674.

*EAA Chapter 75 Glider Club, Lat. 40°36'00", Long. 90°51'41", 1½ miles south on I-80, Exit 280 (702 8th St., Durant 52747); (319) 785-4830.

Omaha Soaring Society, Inc., North Omaha Airport, 2 miles north on 72nd St. (PO Box 403, Council Bluffs 51502); (712) 366-1330.

Silent Knights, Inc., Ames Municipal Airport, south edge of City on Airport Rd. (c/o J. F. Smith, RR 3, Ames 50010); (515) 232-3013.

KANSAS Air Capital Soaring Enterprises, Wichita Gliderport, 1½ miles east of Greenwich Rd. on 45th St. N (13501 E 45th St. N, Wichita 67228); (316) 733-1702, 733-2213.

*Kansas Soaring Association, Sunflower Aerodrome, west of Yoder, south of Hutchinson (c/o Tonk Mills, 115 N Crestway, Wichita 67208); (316) 663-7232 or 722-2183.

Mesa Verde Airport, 12 miles north of I-70 on Hwy. 75, 9 miles north of Topeka (c/o J. W. Brewer, 502 W 18th St., lot 1, Junction City 66441).

KENTUCKY Central Kentucky Soaring, Inc., Madison Airport, 7 miles south-southeast of Richmond (c/o D. K. Walker, Rt. 4, PO Box 178, Irvine 40336); (606) 723-3961.

*Louisville Soaring Club, Inc., Shelbyville (8132 Lake Terrace #12, Louisville 40222); (502) 426-5476.

LOUISIANA Aero Nutz, Inc., Huenefeld Airport, 3 miles east of Monroe Regional Airport, US 80 (PO Box 4151, Monroe 71201); (318) 325-7797.

*Central Louisiana Soaring Society, Inc., Summerville Airport, 10 miles south of Alexandria on Hwy. 76 at Chambers (c/o H. A. Miller, 5812 Hiawatha St., Alexandria 71301); (318) 448-3197.

Louisiana Soaring Center, Oak Hill Gliderport, 6 miles north of US Hwy. 190 on LA 445 (PO Box 1173, Covington 70433); (504) 892-1629 or 345-5816.

MAINE   Turner Soaring, Twitchell's Airport, 6 miles north of Auburn (Rt. 4, Turner); (207) 225-3490.

MARYLAND   Cumberland Soaring Group, Cumberland Maryland Municipal Airport (PO Box 866, Cumberland 21502); (304) 738-9118 or 738-9670 and (301) 729-2886.

MASSACHUSETTS

Berkshire Soaring Society, Inc., Pittsfield Airport, 2 miles southwest of Pittsfield (Tom King, 47 East St., Dalton); (413) 634-5581.

Gliding Club of Boston, Plymouth Airport, Plymouth, Rt. 3 to Exit 6, 4 miles west (Plymouth Airport, Plymouth 02360); (617) 746-7337.

*Greater Boston Soaring Club, Inc., Sterling Airport, Rt. 12 (Greenland Rd.), south of Sterling (74 Warren Rd., Sudbury, MA); (617) 422-8836 or 422-9784.

*MIT Soaring Association, Mansfield, 25 miles south of Boston, Intersection of I-95 and 495 (c/o C. Flagg, 22 King Philip Rd., Sudbury 01776); (617) 443-3706.

*Mohawk Soaring Club, Harriman Airport, Rt. 2, between Williamstown and North Adams, MA (250 Alplaus Ave., Alplaus 12008); (413) 664-9051 and (518) 372-5248, 399-0589 or 399-0700.

*New England Soaring Association, Barre-Hiller Airport, Barre; (617) 332-5075.

MICHIGAN   *Adrian Soaring Club, Inc., Lenawee County Airport, 2 miles southwest of Adrian (34218 Cass Court, Farmington 48024); (313) 477-5057.

Benz Aviation, Iona Airport, between Lansing and Grand Rapids off I-96, north on M-66 for 4 miles, right to Iona Airport (3148 South State Rd., Iona Airport 48846); (616) 427-9070 or 527-0979.

*Huron Valley Soaring, Inc., Cackleberry Airport, Hamburg (c/o Paul Summers, 3166 Lexington, Ann Arbor 48105); (313) 761-7974.

*Northwest Soaring Club of Frankfort, Frankfort Airport, ¾ mile east of Frankfort (PO Box 88, Frankfort 49635); (616) 352-7623 or 882-4303.

*Vultures, Inc., Oxford, 3½ miles north of Oxford on M-24 (c/o Robert Williams, 760 Ranveen Dr., Union Lake 48085); (313) 698-2216 or 628-9097.

MINNESOTA *Minnesota Association of Soaring Clubs (c/o Harris W. Holler, 3901 Harriet Ave., Minneapolis 55409); (612) 822-5605.

*Minnesota Soaring Club, Carleton Airport, 35 miles south of St. Paul at the junction of Hwy. 56 and Hwy. 19 (c/o Dale A. Fletcher, 12 Irvine Park, St. Paul 55102); (507) 645-4030.

*Red Wing Soaring Association, Benson's Airport, 2 miles north of White Bear Lake on Hwy. 61 (1648 Fernwood St., St. Paul 55108); (612) 489-6519 or 645-9678.

*St. Croix Soaring, Osceola, Wisconsin, from Minneapolis-St. Paul area, I-35 to 97, go east to Minn. 95, then north to Minn. 243, turn east to Osceola; airport 1 mile south of town (c/o Lee Bradshaw, 17604 Notre Dame St., Forest Lake, Minn. 55025); (612) 464-8264 or 429-3706.

Soar, Inc., Owatonna Municipal Airport, 2 miles north-northwest of Owatonna, I-35 (PO Box 199, Owatonna 55060); (507) 451-6611.

MISSISSIPPI Bay Aviation, Inc., Stennis International Airport, Bay St. Louis (Rt. 3, PO Box 987, Bay St. Louis 39520); (601) 467-5434.

State College Glider Club, Starkville, Bryan Airport, 1 mile west of town (Drawer A, Mississippi State Univ. 39762); (601) 325-3623.

MISSOURI Capital Soaring, Inc., Memorial Airport, north of Missouri River (PO Box 515, Jefferson City 65102); (314) 636-7239.

*Central Missouri Soaring Society, 4849 St. Charles Rd., Columbia 65201; (314) 474-6967.

*Midwestern Soaring Association, Inc., East Kansas City Airport, Grain Valley, 17 miles east of Kansas City on I-70 (c/o 16305 E 31st, Independence 64055); (816) 361-4996.

St. Charles Flying Service, St. Charles Airport, Hwy. 5 (3001 Airport Rd., St. Charles 63301); (314) 946-6066.

*St. Louis Soaring Association, Highland-Winet Airport, Highland, IL, 1 mile east of Highland on Rt. 40 (4055 Chartley Dr., Bridgeton 63044); (314) 644-1027.

MONTANA   Bridger Mountain Soaring, Gallatin Field, 8 miles northwest of Bozeman, Hwy. 10 (PO Box 808, Belgrade 59714); (406) 388-4804.

Red Lodge Airways, Red Lodge Airport, ½ mile west of Red Lodge (PO Box 909, Red Lodge 59068); (406) 446-2319 or 446-2118.

NEBRASKA   Frelin Soaring Association, Lincoln Municipal Airport (PO Box 83208, Lincoln 68501); (402) 423-6116 or 489-7334.

Panhandle Soarers, Inc., Scottsbluff Airport, 3 miles east of Scottsbluff (c/o William B. Heilig, 3610 Ave. D, Scottsbluff 69361); (308) 632-8184.

Sioux Air, Inc., Martin Airport, 2 miles west of South Sioux City (PO Box 425, South Sioux City 68776); (402) 494-3667.

NEVADA   *Air Sailing, Inc., Air Sailing Gliderport, Palimino Valley, 15 miles north of Sparks on Rt. 33, left on Winnemucca Ranch Rd. for 6 miles (PO Box 3368, San Mateo, CA 94403); (415) 593-7986.

Desert Soaring of Boulder City, Boulder City Airport, between Las Vegas and Hoover Dam on Boulder Hwy. 95 (PO Box 637, Boulder City 89005); (702) 293-4577 or 565-6914.

Minden Tahoe Aviation, Douglas County Airport, Airport Rd. off 395 (PO Box 1119, Minden 89423); (702) 782-4569 or 883-4569.

*Nevada Soaring Association, Inc., Air Sailing, Inc., 30 miles north of Sparks on Pyramid Lake Hwy. (1200 W 12th St., Reno 89503); (702) 747-0870.

Sierra-Nevada Soaring, Reno-Stead Airport, 11 miles northwest of Reno on Hwy. 395 (PO Box 60036, Reno 89506); (702) 972-7757 or 322-1421.

Silver State Soaring, Inc., Air Sailing Gliderport, 15 miles north of Sparks off Rt. 33A, left on Winnemucca Ranch Rd., 5 miles to access road (Star Route 1, Winnemucca Ranch Rd., Reno 89510); (702) 329-4652.

Terra Training, Jean, Nevada, 20 miles south of Las Vegas (5616 South Haven, Las Vegas 89119); (702) 739-6111.

NEW HAMPSHIRE

Franconia Aviation, Franconia Inn Airport, 2.7 miles from Franconia Village (c/o Franconia Inn, Franconia 03580); (603) 823-5542.

*Kearsage Soaring Association, Inc., Eagles Nest, New London, Exit 11 off Rt. 89, 2 miles east on Rt. 11 (Crockett's Corner, New London 03257); (617) 746-3001 or 526-4219.

*Mt. Washington Soaring Association, Inc., North Conway, New Hampshire, 2 miles south of town on Rt. 16 (46 Leewood Rd., Wellesley, MA 02181); (617) 235-8467.

Northeastern Gliderport, Brady Ave., Salem, NH, I-93N, Exit 1, turn right at first light and again at next light (NE Light A/C Inc., PO Box 252, Lynn, MA 01903); (603) 898-7919.

NEW JERSEY Airborne Arts, Inc., Sky Manor Airport, Pittstown, 5 miles south from Exit 12 off I-78, Rt. 513 to Pittstown, Pittstown Rd. to Sky Manor Airport (RD 2, PO Box 22A, Pittstown 08867); (201) 996-6772.

*Central Jersey Soaring Club, Trenton-Robbinsville Airport, NJ Turnpike, Exit 7A (c/o R. Bowman, 31 Rolling Ln., Hamilton Square 08690); (609) 587-7530.

*Icarus Soaring Club, Blairstown, 5 miles east of Delaware Water Gap on Rt. 94 (117 Johnston Dr., Wachung 07060); (201) 754-0018.

Soaring Society of Princeton University, Forrestal Airport, east side of US 1, 1 mile north of Princeton (SSPU Flight Research Lab, Forrestal Campus, Princeton 08544).

*South Jersey Soaring Society, Hammonton Municipal, north on Rt. 206 for 2 miles, then east for 1 mile (489 Weymouth Rd., Vineland 08320, Otto Zauner); (609) 697-0950.

Tocks Island Soaring, Inc., Blairstown Airport, 7 miles from town, north on I-80 (Blairstown Airport 07825); (201) 362-8311 or 667-9234.

Valley Soaring, Randall Airport, Middletown, NY, NY 17 west to Exit 122A (Middletown Rd.) to Golf Course Rd., left to Mc-Manus, right to airport (42 Lenape Trail, Wayne 07470); (201) 696-8823 and (914) 343-9491.

NEW MEXICO

*Albuquerque Soaring Club, Moriarty Airport, 1½ miles south and 2 miles east of Moriarty (PO Box 11254, Albuquerque 87192); (505) 298-1507 or 832-9921.

*El Paso Soaring Society, Las Cruces Municipal Airport, 3 miles west of Las Cruces on I-10 (PO Box 13281, El Paso, TX 79912); (915) 584-3249.

*Hobbs Soaring Society, Hobbs Industrial Air Park, 5 miles north of Hobbs on Lovington Hwy. (PO Box 831, Hobbs 88240); (505) 393-2153 or 392-4971.

NEW YORK   Aero Soaring Club, Dart Airport, 2 miles east of Mayville on Rt. 17 (PO Box 107, Mayville 14757); (716) 753-2111.

Catskill Valley Flying Service, Freehold Airport, 7/10 mile from Freehold, Rt. 32 (PO Box 44, South Cairo 12482); (518) 634-7626 or 622-3307.

*Chautauqua Soaring Society, Inc., Chautauqua County Airport, West Oak Hill Rd., Jamestown (PO Box 116, Maple Springs 14756); (716) 386-3108.

Gilad Soaring Service, Kamp Airport, Durhamville, north of Oneida, halfway between Syracuse and Utica, Rt. 46N from Oneida to Rt. 31E, 1 mile east of intersection (66 Root St., New Hartford 13413); (315) 363-1980 or 735-3643.

*Harris Hill Soaring Corporation, Harris Hill (RD 1, Harris Hill, Elmira 14903); (607) 734-0641, 734-3128.

*Iroquois Soaring Association, Cooperstown-Westville Airport, 7 miles southeast of Cooperstown on Rt. 166 (PO Box 292, Cooperstown 13326); (607) 286-3373.

*Ithaca Soaring Club, 5 miles west of Ithaca on Rt. 79 (1755 Mecklenburg Rd., Ithaca 14850); (607) 272-6087.

*Long Island Soaring Association, Brookhaven Airport, William-Floyd Pkwy. and Sunrise Hwy. (222 Grand, Shirley 11967); (516) 997-5575.

*Mohawk Soaring Club, Saratoga County Airport, south on Rt. 50 from Saratoga Springs, left on county road opposite Saratoga Performing Arts Center (250 Alplaus Ave., Alplaus 12008); (518) 399-0700, 372-5248, or 399-0589.

*Niagara Soaring Club, Inc., Lockport-Cambria Airport, Vandusen Rd., 4 miles northwest of Lockport (c/o Donald G. Hobel, 3767 Moyer Rd., North Tonawanda 14120); (716) 693-1823 or 731-3603.

Perrucci Aviation, Tri-Cities Airport, 1 mile west of Endicott off Rt. 17C (310 E Main St., Endicott 13760); (607) 785-1191.

*Rochester Soaring Club, Dansville Airport, north edge of Dansville (15 Tuxford Rd., Pittsford 14534); (716) 381-6983.

Sailflights, Inc., Wurtsboro Airport, 3 miles north of Wurtsboro on Rt. 209 (Wurtsboro Airport, Wurtsboro 12790); (914) 888-2791.

Sky Sailors, Inc., Brookhaven Airport, Sunrise Hwy. and William Floyd Pkwy. (222 Grand Ave., Shirley 11967); (516) 281-6565.

*Soaring Club of Syracuse, Inc., Kamp Airport, ¾ mile south of Rt. 31, west side of Irish Ridge Rd. in Durham (512 Oswego St., Liverpool 13088); (315) 457-2561.

Thermal Ridge Soaring, Inc., Therman Ridge Gliderport, Preble, Rt. 11, 3 miles south of Tully (115 Kittell Rd., Fayetteville 13066); (315) 446-3790 or 446-4545.

*Triple Cities Soaring Society, Tri-Cities Airport, Rt. 17 to Endicott, west on Rt. 17C, Endicott 13760; (607) 785-0988.

Valley Soaring, Randall Airport, Middletown, Rt. 17 to Exit 122A, out E Main to Golf Course and turn left, turn right at

McMann's Place (42 Lenape Trail, Wayne, NJ 07470); (201) 696-8823.

Wurtsboro Flight Service, Inc., Wurtsboro Airport, 2 miles northeast of Wurtsboro on Rt. 209 (RD 1, Wurtsboro Airport, Wurtsboro 12790); (914) 888-2791.

NORTH CAROLINA

Meadowlark Soaring, Inc., Meadowlark Gliderport, 2 miles north of Franklinton (PO Box 2006, Chapel Hill 27514); (919) 929-3404.

*NCSU Soaring Club, Meadowlark Gliderport, 2 miles north of Franklinton (North Carolina State Univ. Soaring Club, Mech. & Aerospace Engr., PO Box 5246, Raleigh 27650); (919) 737-2360.

Stanly Soaring School, Inc., Anson County Airport, 5 miles north of Wadesboro on US 52 (508 N Ninth St., Albemarle 28001); (704) 983-1726 or 694-2516.

NORTH DAKOTA

*University of North Dakota Soaring, Thompson, 7 miles south-southeast of Grand Forks International Airport (PO Box 8216, Univ. Station, Grand Forks 58201); (701) 777-2791.

OHIO   *Bryan Soaring Club, Woodruff Field, Montpelier, 1 mile east of Montpelier (915 Lemonwood Ct., Ft. Wayne, IN 46825); (219) 489-4732 and (419) 485-3716.

*Caesar Creek Soaring Club, Caesar Creek Gliderport, 4 miles south of Waynesville off I-71 (PO Box 581, Wright Brothers Branch, Dayton 45409); (513) 434-3953.

*Canton-Akron Soaring Club, Wadsworth Municipal Airport, 1 mile south on Rt. 57, 10 miles west of Akron (710 Mentor Rd., Akron 44303); (216) 864-9114.

*Central Ohio Soaring Association, Marion Municipal Airport, 3 miles northeast of Marion off Rt. 23, east on Williamsport Rd. (5288 Butternut Ct. W, Columbus 43229); (614) 888-1987.

*Cleveland Soaring Society, Liberty Airpark, 9 miles east of Streetsboro (c/o 6158 S.R. 303, Ravenna 44206); (216) 296-9702.

Elf Soaring Enterprises, Woodruff Field, off County Rd. 13,

south of Rt. 107 (RR 3, Airport Rd., Montpelier 43543); (419) 485-3716.

*Fun Country Soaring, Inc., Botsford Airport, east edge of Wellington on State Rt. 18 (c/o Airport, RFD 2, Wellington 44090); (216) 988-2791.

Lane's Lebanon Air Service, Inc., Lebanon-Warren County Airport, 3 miles west-northwest of Lebanon (2460 Greentree Rd., Lebanon 45036); (513) 932-7966.

*Northern Ohio Soaring Association, Price Airport, 3 miles south of Youngstown Airport, 1 mile west of Rt. 193 (c/o Alfred J. Davis, 418 Williams St., Niles 44446); (216) 652-4861.

*Sky Roamers Soaring Club, Botsford Airport, Rt. 18, ¼ mile east of Wellington (1676 Dorchester Dr., Brunswick 44212); (216) 225-1353.

OKLAHOMA Oklahoma State University Aviation Education Department, Stillwater Municipal Airport, 1 mile west of Hwy. 177H on Airport Rd. (Stillwater 74074); (405) 572-7881 or 377-8406.

Silent Flight Soaring School, Mustang Field, El Reno, 20 miles west of Oklahoma City, Exit I-40 at country club (1431 Galen St., Norman 73069); (405) 321-4000.

*Southwest Oklahoma Soaring Association, Sky Harbor Airport, 4 miles south of Chattanooga (PO Box 1663, Lawton 73502); (405) 353-3896 or 353-7575.

*Tulsa Skyhawks Soaring Club, Inc., Haskell Airport, 30 miles east of Tulsa (PO Box 1345, Tulsa 74101); (918) 936-2387.

OREGON *Emerald Valley Soaring Club, Daniels Field, Harrisburg, 20 miles north of Eugene at I-5, second Harrisburg Interchange (86436 Needham Rd., Eugene 97405); (503) 683-4931.

*SAIL-EM GLIDERS, INC., Independence State Airport, 1 mile northwest from downtown Independence (2825 Wiletta, Suite B, Albany 97321); (503) 926-8871 or 581-7979.

*Willamette Valley Soaring Club, North Plains Gliderport (private), Hillsboro, 20 miles west on Hwy. 26 from Portland (Henry Hillman, 3356 Southwest Fairmont Blvd., Portland 97201); (503) 227-2019 or 642-3373.

PENNSYLVANIA

Beltville Airport, 4 miles east of Lehighton off Rt. 209 (PO Box 171, RD 3, Lehighton 18235); (215) 377-9914 or 377-4887.

*Brandywine Soaring Association, New Garden Field, Touchkenamon, Rt. 1 and Rt. 41, between Avondale and Kennett Sq., 15 miles north-northwest of Wilmington (PO Box 454, Wilmington, Delaware 19899); (302) 654-0536.

*Cloudniners, Inc., Brandywine Airport, Airport Rd., West Chester (PO Box 262, Exton 19341); (215) 644-9620.

*Kittatinny Soaring Club, Stroudsburg-Pocono Airport, Exit 52 off US 80, 2 miles out on Bus 209 north of East Stroudsburg (908 White St., Stroudsburg 18360); (717) 424-8551 or 424-1872.

Kutztown Aviations Service, Inc., Kutztown Airport, next to Kutztown State College (Rt. 1, PO Box 1, Kutztown 19530); (215) 683-3821 or 683-8389.

*Mid-Atlantic Soaring Association, Inc., Frederick, Maryland and Fairfield, PA (M-ASA, 4823 Teen Barnes Rd., Frederick, MD 21701); (301) 663-9753.

Mifflin County Sailplane Association (c/o W. Haubert, PO Box 205, Mexico 17056).

North Star Aerosports, Inc., Stroudsburg-Pocono Airport, Exit 52 off US 80, Bus. 209 north 2 miles, near Delaware Water Gap and New Jersey–Pennsylvania Ridge (PO Box 201, East Stroudsburg 18301); (717) 424-1872.

*Philadelphia Glider Council, Hilltown, 4½ miles north on US 202 from Chalfont on PA 152 (934 Rt. 152, Perkasie 18944); (215) 822-9974.

*Pittsburgh Soaring Club, Bandel Airport, 10 miles east of Washington County Airport (c/o Bruno Carceo, 162 Aria Dr., Pittsburgh 15220); (412) 945-6121.

Posey Aviation, Van Sant Airport, 2 miles southwest of Erwinna (PO Box 41, Erwinna 18920); (215) 847-2770.

Ridge Soaring, Inc., Bald Eagle Ridge Gliderport, 9 miles south of I-80 on Rt. 220 S (RD, Julian 16844); (814) 355-1792.

*The Soaring Dutchmen, Beltzville Airport, RD 3, Lehighton, 2 miles north on US 209 from Exit 34 of northeast extension of Pennsylvania turnpike (c/o L. W. Homeier, Greenbank Rd., Rosemont 19010); (215) 972-6888.

RHODE ISLAND

*Brown Soaring Club, Inc., North Central Airport, Lincoln (Student Activities Office, PO Box 15, Brown University, Providence 02912); (401) 333-1212.

SOUTH CAROLINA

*Aiken Soaring Club, Aiken Airport, US 1, 1 mile south on I-20 (c/o R. S. Olcott, 106 Idlewild Dr., Aiken 29801); (803) 649-2764.

Bermuda High Soaring School, Inc., Chester Airport, 6 miles north of Chester (PO Box 809, Chester 29706); (803) 385-6061.

Carolina Sailplanes, Inc., Cypress Bay Airport, Hwy. 17, Little River (PO Box 241, Little River 29566); (803) 249-4523.

Tarheel Soaring Club, Inc., Chester Airport (David York); (919) 621-0165.

SOUTH DAKOTA   No soaring sites currently operating in this state.

TENNESSEE

Chilhowee Gliderport, 5 miles north of Benton on Hwy. 411 (15 Fairhills Dr., Chattanooga 37415); (615) 338-2000 or 266-1767.

Eagleville Soaring, Puckett Field, 4 miles south of Eagleville on Hwy. 41 (1311 Currey Rd., Nashville 37417); (615) 274-6341.

*Memphis Soaring Society, Inc., Colonial Airport, 3 miles east of Olive Branch (c/o 232 S Yates Rd., Memphis 38117); (901) 683-9458.

TEXAS   Aero-Country Aviation, Inc., Aero-Country Airport, 8 miles west of McKinney (Rt. 1, Rockhill Rd., McKinney 75069); (512) 347-2416 or 248-6410.

Airmarc Aviation, Schlemeyer Field, Andrews High, 2 miles north of Odessa (7000 Andrews High, Odessa 79762); (915) 367-9141, 9142, or 9143.

Alamo Soaring, Inc., Castroville Airport, Hwy. 90 West, 14 miles west of San Antonio (PO Box 793, Castroville 78009); (512) 653-2294, 538-2828, or 822-6050.

*Fault Line Flyers, Georgetown Municipal Airport, 3 miles

northwest of Georgetown (Floyd Bates, 1110 Bruton Springs Rd., Austin 78746); (512) 263-2233.

*High Plains Soaring Society, Air Sport Canyon, 4 miles south of Lanyon, 1 mile east (PO Box 604, Amarillo 79105); (806) 372-3521.

Houston Soaring Association, Inc., Katy Airport, Katy, I-10 west to Exit 742, turn right at Ave. D then 8 miles (7435 Jackwood, Houston 77074); (713) 771-4246.

Hunt Pan Am Distributors, Brown and Brown Aviation, Weslaco (PO Box 706, Brownsville 78520); (512) 542-9111 or 968-9361.

*Mesilla Valley Soaring Society, Katy Airport, Katy, see T/H Enterprises for directions (415 Bayou View, Seabrook 77586); (713) 334-1764.

*North Dallas Gliders, Hartlee Airport, 3 miles northeast of Denton (c/o R. C. Gibbons, 709 Parkview Circle, Richardson 75080).

*Soaring Club of Houston, Inc., Sky Lakes Airfield, Waller Country Club, 4 miles south of Waller on FM 362 (c/o 14527 Carolcrest, Houston 77079); (713) 497-7586.

Southwest Soaring, Inc., Caddo Mills Airport, 30 miles east of Dallas on I-30, go north 2 miles on FM 1565 (PO Box 460, Caddo Mills 75005); (214) 527-3124.

*Texas Soaring Association, 7 miles south of Midlothian, south on FM 663, west on FM 875 to first road, then south for 2 miles (PO Box 1069, Midlothian 76065); (214) 775-8803.

T/H Enterprises, Inc., Katy Airport, Katy, I-10 west to exit 742, turn right at Ave. D then 8 miles (7435 Jackwood, Houston 77074); (713) 771-4246.

Vanair Aviation Services, Rooke Field, 2½ miles south of Refugio (PO Box 637, Woodsboro 78393); (512) 526-4241.

Windermere Soaring School, Windermere Gliderport, 30 miles west of Austin off Hwy. 71 (Rt. 2, Box 491, Spicewood 78669); (512) 693-4663 or 327-3230.

UTAH *Brigham Soaring Association, Inc., Brigham City Municipal Airport, 60 miles north of Salt Lake City on I-15 (964 Englewood Dr., Brigham City 84302); (801) 723-2259 or 723-8833.

Heber Valley Flying Service, Inc., Heber Valley Airport, 1 mile south of Heber City (Rt. 1, PO Box 443A, Heber City 84032); (801) 654-2061.

Soaring Society of Utah, Heber City Airport (4589 Wallace Lane, Salt Lake City 84117); (801) 277-9984.

*Utah Soaring Association, Heber Valley Airport, south end of Heber City on Hwy. 189 (PO Box 1676, Salt Lake City 84110); (801) 532-1481.

VERMONT Green Mountain, Springfield Airport (Springfield-Hartness Airport, Springfield 06156).

Mansfield Aviation, Inc., Morrisville–Stowe State Airport, Rt. 100 north from Hwy. 89 (Morrisville 05661); (802) 888-5150.

Stowe Soaring, Morrisville–Stowe State Airport, 3 miles south to Morrisville on Rt. 100 (Morrisville 05661); (802) 888-5150.

Post Mills Aviation, Inc., Post Mills Airport, 15 miles north of Hanover, Exit 14 off Rt. I-89, Rt. 113 to Post Mills Village (PO Box 51, Post Mills 05058); (802) 333-9254.

Sugarbush Soaring Association, Warren-Sugarbush Airport, east of Rt. 100, Warren (PO Box 123, Warren 05674); (802) 496-2290 or 496-4188.

VIRGINIA National Capital Soaring Association, Warrenton Air Park, 2 miles south of Warrenton, Rt. 29 (1111 Army Navy Dr. #C1209, Arlington); (703) 979-6498.

New River Soaring Association, Ltd., New River Valley Airport, Dublin, Rt. 81 to Dublin Exit, north on 100 for 5 miles (c/o Frank L. Miller, Rt. 4, PO Box 311, Salem 24153); (703) 389-3227.

*Ridge and Valley Soaring Club, L. B. Gilderport, Lexington, just south of Lexington off Rt. 11 (c/o Rohmann's Univ. Sport Shop, 1525 University Ave., Charlottesville 22903); (804) 298-7561.

Soaring Unlimited, Inc., Chesterfield County Airport, 15 miles southwest of Richmond (7400 Whitepine Rd., Richmond 23234); (804) 271-0465.

Tidewater Soaring Society, Inc., Garner Airport, 5 miles northeast of Windsor on Rt. 605 1/10 mile west of Rt. 637 intersection (PO Box 86, Rt. 2, Windsor 23487); (804) 357-3948.

Warrenton Soaring Center, Warrenton Airpark, 3.5 miles south of town, Rt. 29, left on Rt. 616 (PO Box 118, Warrenton 22186); (703) 347-0054.

WASHINGTON

Cascade Wave Flights West, Madras, Oregon, 2 miles north of Madras on US 26 (3010 NE 44 St., Vancouver 98663); (206) 695-3337 or 694-8905.

Eastern Evergreen Enterprises, Inc., Moses Lake Municipal Airport, 2½ miles north of town (1122 Baker, Moses Lake 98837); (509) 765-6400.

Flight Incorporated, Richland Airport, on bypass Hwy., look for signs (1986 Marshall, Richland 99352); (509) 946-7746.

*Jet Aero and Free Air Falconeers, Colville Airport, 1 mile north of Colville (625 S Rae St., Colville 9914); (509) 684-5162.

Lesley's Sky Sailing, call or write for location (PO Box 2661, Spokane 99220); (509) 747-4720.

*Seattle Glider Council, Inc., Ephrata Airport, 1 mile south of town (c/o Bob Chase, 12422 68th Ave. NE, Kirkland 98033); (206) 823-6500.

Soaring Unlimited, Inc., Skyport, ½ mile west of Issaquah on I-90, 15 miles east of Seattle (PO Box 548, Kirkland 98033); (206) 454-2514.

WEST VIRGINIA

*Mountaineer Soaring Association, Inc., Robert Newlon Field, 6 miles east of Huntington, off Rt. 2 (1 Reeves Dr., Nitro 25143); (304) 727-9901 or 346-4710.

WISCONSIN

*Aerospace Explorer Post 309, West Bend Municipal Airport, 3 miles east of West Bend (2501 E Newton Ave., Milwaukee 53211); Paul Hammersmith (414) 962-6727. (Membership for teenage pilots & students.)

*Monona Glider Club, Lodi, 30 miles north of Madison (215 Frost Woods Rd., Monona 53716); (608) 222-3142.

Silent Wings, Inc., Aero Park Airport, Hampton Ave. west from Milwaukee (W 204, N 5022, Lannon Rd., Aero Park Airport, Menomonee Falls 53051); (414) 252-9992.

*Thermal Sniffers Soaring Club, West Bend Municipal Airport 3 miles east of city on Hwy. 33 (5007 N Bay Ridge Ave., Whitefish Bay 53217); (414) 962-1340.

West Bend Flying Service, West Bend, 3 miles east of city (PO Box 409, West Bend 53095); (414) 334-5603.

WYOMING   No soaring sites currently operating in this state.

FURTHER READING

Dozens of soaring books ranging from introductory material to the technical, are listed in each issue of *Soaring* magazine. We suggest the following brief reading list for the serious student pilot. Some of the books can be ordered through your local bookstore, others by writing to The Soaring Society of America, Inc., PO Box 66071, Los Angeles, CA 90066.

America's Soaring Book. Flying magazine editors. New York: Charles Scribner's Sons, 1974. A comprehensive collection of sailplanes, prominent pilots and soaring records.

American Soaring Handbook. Los Angeles: Soaring Society of America, Inc., 1965. Ten booklets under separate titles, from history to maintenance and repair; available in a set or individually.

Conway, Carle. *The Joy of Soaring.* Los Angeles: Soaring Society of America, Inc., 1969. Standard flight training manual sanctioned by the SSA and used for over ten years.

Piggott, Derek. *Beginning Gliding.* New York: Barnes and Noble, 1977. An introduction to soaring flight.

Reichmann, Helmut A. *Cross-Country Soaring.* Santa Monica, California: Graham Thomson, Ltd., 1978. An advanced study of cross-country techniques.

Soaring Flight Manual. Soaring Society of America, Review Committee. Denver: Jeppesen Sanderson, Inc., 1978. Ground school textbook with workbook and practice FAA exam.

Soaring in America. Los Angeles: Soaring Society of America, Inc., 1979. Introductory booklet with basic information for newcomers.

Wallington, C. E. *Meteorology for Glider Pilots.* London: John Murray, Ltd., 1977. A comprehensive study of soaring weather.

Wolters, Richard A. *The Art and Technique of Soaring.* New York: McGraw-Hill, 1971. A flight training manual with outstanding photographs.

Wolters, Richard A. *Once upon a Thermal.* Los Angeles: Soaring Society of America, Inc., 1974. A popular, humorous account of one pilot's soaring career.

Linda Morrow, who grew up in Arizona, is an English instructor at Pasadena City College and a student sailplane pilot. Ray, a native Californian, is a mechanical engineer in charge of research and engineering for a dental manufacturing company. He is a licensed soaring pilot and has long been interested in boats, cars and aircraft. The Morrows' interest in soaring dates to 1965 when they were traveling in Bavaria, and watched a sailplane land in an Alpine meadow. Now they fly sailplanes on weekends in the Mojave desert, and share pleasure in the sport with their young daughter, Kim and son, Chris. The Morrows live in Arcadia, California.